JESSICA MARTIN

Holiness and Desire

CANTERBURY
PRESS
Norwich

© Jessica Martin 2020

First published in 2020 by the Canterbury Press Norwich
Editorial office
3rd Floor, Invicta House
108–114 Golden Lane
London EC1Y OTG, UK
www.canterburypress.co.uk

Canterbury Press is an imprint of Hymns Ancient & Modern Ltd
(a registered charity)

Hymns Ancient & Modern® is a registered trademark of
Hymns Ancient & Modern Ltd
13a Hellesdon Park Road, Norwich,
Norfolk NR6 5DR, UK

British Library Cataloguing in Publication data

A catalogue record for this book is available
from the British Library

978 1 78622 126 1

Typeset by Manila Typesetting Company
Printed and bound in Great Britain by
CPI Group (UK) Ltd

Wants are the bands and ligatures between God and us. Had we not wanted, we could never have been obliged. Whereas now we are infinitely obliged, because we want infinitely. From Eternity it was requisite that we should want. We could never else have enjoyed anything: Our own wants are treasures. And if want be a treasure, sure everything is so.

Thomas Traherne, *Centuries of Meditations*

Dedication

To my mother, Bernice Martin,
of whose 1981 book *A Sociology of
Contemporary Cultural Change*
this is an admiring continuation

and in memory of

David Martin
30 June 1929 – 8 March 2019

Contents

Acknowledgements

Without friends and readers, this book would have remained as unfinished as the many other writing projects that were in the end swallowed up by life. To those friends and readers – who gave time they could not really afford and conversed so intelligently with the text – I am deeply obliged. To Nicola Bown, Andrew Brown, Fenella Cannell; to members of the Ely theological group Concord; to Maria Farrell, Catherine Fox, Alan Jacobs, Victoria Johnson, Helen King, Rachel Mann, Sarah Perry. To my mother, Bernice Martin, who taught me to think; to my brothers Jonathan, Izaak and Magnus, who played so much of the music. To Stella Martin, to whom the promises of desire have over and over again not been kind, and yet manages to stay kind herself. To Anne Richards, Rowan Williams, Ross Wilson. To Chris Rowland, who made it possible to look at fearful things.

And especially to my husband Francis Spufford, who has shown me that ruthlessness and obstinacy can be virtues; without whose attention and generosity there would be no book at all; without whom I would be more strange to the disciplines of love.

With thee conversing I forget all time.

To the Reader

Perhaps you picked this book up expecting to read some theology. Perhaps you are hoping that it will speak helpfully – or at any rate clearly – into the debates current in the Church of England over sexuality. Perhaps you like the title. Perhaps you are curious about culture criticism, or literature. Perhaps you have questions about how the Bible can address the dilemmas of modern living. You might be – I hope you are – really interested in what it could be to live well and expectantly in dark times. All these things are discussed here, not separately but together, because each one of them is a different mode for expressing human desire and its relationship to the call to holiness. And that's what the whole book is about.

This is a really, really wide range of inquiry, so I've gone for an unusual approach, one that is more like an old-fashioned 'essay' than a modern 'argument'. It uses all kinds of different ways of thinking: from culture criticism to my own life story, from biblical interpretation to thinking about adverts, games and videos; from social-scientific surveys to poetry, novels, films. I do address the issues on sexuality that concern the Church, issues finding their points of collision in same-sex relationships and gender identity. But I don't think it is helpful to focus on these issues in isolation, because I believe that they are being required to take much more cultural freight than is fair, right or true.

So if your main reason for reading is to find out what I think the Christian view of same-sex marriage should be, and why I think it, then you will find out, but as part of a piece of thinking about what a distinctive holiness might look like for *everybody* – not just people who don't fit into the heterosexual mould – within the shaping and indeed distorting pressures of our highly sexualized modern culture. I've taken the whole vista of modern desire, not only the sexual kind but everything that animates human longing, and I've looked at what our culture is doing with it. This is a book for everyone who has thought that there might be something wrong with our default assumptions about human nature and sexuality, but can't quite work out what.

And what you have in your hands is a personal view. I use the experience of my own lifetime, a lifetime that has spanned enormous cultural change. I've deployed a huge variety of sources, from the Bible to social media. It's all woven together into the particular viewpoint of this middle-aged, white, heterosexual woman with a suburban English background who is Christian by confession and by conviction. The poems and so on that I have chosen have been the ones influencing my life. Some are very well known; some are fairly obscure. Some appear as a fleeting reference or quotation; others are discussed quite carefully. All will, I hope, speak for themselves without readers having to have prior knowledge of them.

Parts of the book may even be quite fun.

A quick word about the book's shape. First, you can't think about Christian holiness without thinking about the Bible. So the book begins with a one-chapter section called 'Scripture'. This talks about scriptural authority and readerly response, and is a kind of grounding for the ways that the Bible will support the rest of the book. (But if you want to go straight to the discussion on desire in Part 2, it will make perfect sense without reading this section.)

The middle section of the book, 'Desire', is, if you like, the main course. It comes in four chapters called 'Longing', 'Looking', 'Joining' and 'Self-Fashioning'. 'Longing' sets the scene, drawing out the relationship between human wanting and the desire for God, and how it's hidden or frustrated or distracted by modern secular attitudes to desire. The next chapter, 'Looking', focuses down on the traditional preliminaries of desire, the action of looking at someone (or something) and wanting it. It thinks about what that might mean in a world dominated by screens that allow you to look at people who can't look at you. 'Joining' moves on from looking to doing, to the actions of sexual involvement and the impact of changing cultural expectations around sex and relationships. And 'Self-Fashioning', the last chapter in this section, takes the focus away from relationships with others and looks at modern identity, at the complex relationship between desire and selfhood that particularly preoccupies our society.

The last section, 'Holiness', has two chapters, called 'Converting' and 'Meeting'. In this final section, I suggest ways in which Christians might live faithfully together in spite of all the difficulties that face the project of fidelity. 'Converting' looks at some – perhaps unexpected – contexts for holiness. Last of all, 'Meeting' ends the book, bringing the steadfast love of God together with the desires of his mortal children.

So this is not a guide to a debate. It hopes to go far beyond that. It wants to show why desire and holiness are not enemies; why they need each other; why the things that make up human yearning and the things of God come together, in the end, to make all things new.

One last thing . . .

I wrote this book with my head full of songs. Permissions costs meant that I couldn't quote the lyrics, but without the music the text becomes more dead, white and male in its references than it was when I was thinking it through. There's a Spotify playlist to supply the missing voices at https://open.spotify.com/playlist/67RI7718pbX5Wo5YDF8fHX?si=PWWrwbEKQJ2GWdkeKdwScw (accessed 18.04.2020).

PART I

Scripture

Which thinks about the authority of the Bible
and what kind of relationship humans are invited to
make with it.

I

Reading

Scripture and divine communication

This isn't an 'objective' book. There's no 'God's-eye' view. (Not even God sees that way, anyway.) Objectivity is a child trying to draw God's perspective – but I wasn't planning to attempt it. All the sense I can make is provisional.

But this *is* a book that thinks about the things between humans and God. So I find it utterly necessary to take God's seeing as the foundation, believing that God inhabits the sacred empty space from (and into) which no human eye can look, but by which all human insight must steer: an invisible north. To 'see meaning' with the human eye and brain is to notice a fleeting partial pattern in a fleeting partial way. But that is not all it is. Human knowing – even though it is fragmentary – participates in meaning's divine source and constant changing flow. Someone can be thrown into an epiphany without knowing how it happened or what will happen next.

In another life, I used to teach literature. I helped people to read meaning in written texts. That's just as basic as it sounds – but it wasn't easy or simple. There were real problems with fundamentals. Was meaning part of a great universal truth, or was it always provisional? Should accidental meanings have any weight? Should what an author originally intended matter more than what a reader understands the author to be saying? Do we all understand any given word in a language the same way? How should we deal with the shifting sands of time and context when we consider the life of words and of artefacts made of words? Something that

looked straightforward turned out to have all sorts of perfectly real difficulties.

These problems matter. They matter because everyone
communicates – it's not exactly a specialist thing. And they
don't just apply to literature. They apply to all the ways we
converse. And it turns out that we have to trust each other
for communication to happen at all. You could even say that
communication is a matter of faith. You can't start off every
conversation despairing of your ability to match up what you
mean with what people are going to hear; you have to believe
that true communication is really possible even when the
evidence is often against you.

Relationships keep going because we don't probe too insistently on how agreed our mutual meanings really are. Marriage
breakdown is nearly always characterized by a point when that
faith in shared conversational meanings has broken down too,
when we push sceptically on the terrain of crossover: 'He/she
said *this* but meant *that*.'

You could put all that another way. You could say that
humankind relies upon God to supply meaning in spite of the
many ways our human communications are limited, fractured
and faulty. Yet mostly we don't see why we should thank,
or even acknowledge, his generous underwriting of our local
efforts. In the sixteenth century people believed that language
was a way of seeing God in humanity. The skill of speaking
together with understanding guaranteed civil harmony: it
showed that the 'common good' was always more important
than individual desires.[1] Divine meaning made human communication stable.

The story of the tower of Babel (Genesis 11.1–9) is a weird
thought-experiment which thinks about that. It imagines everyone speaks a single universal language. The people in the story
use their perfect communication powers to threaten heaven:
language makes them gods. Because they forget that they are

---

1 Thomas Wilson, 'Eloquence first Given by God, and after Lost by
Man, and last Repayred by God again', in *The Arte of Rhetorique*, 2nd
edn (London, 1560).

really creatures, God has to remind them: he breaks up their perfect language and they stop understanding each other. So Babel is another 'Fall' story. Its 'take-home' is that human systems of meaning are fractured; our edifices, real and imagined, cannot hold; we need God as a relationship cornerstone. When the apostles speak at Pentecost and everyone hears what they say in their native tongue,[2] it's because the coming of the Spirit brings perfect understanding, earnest of the beautiful order of God's kingdom, uncommonly close. Pentecost underpins not only inspired communication but every intimate relationship.

Because there's another bit to this. Our meaningful communications with each other are *embodied*. Face-to-face we take more information from tone and body language than we do from words. In writing we have sophisticated substitutes for those physical clues in almost all genres. Emojis, for example, attempt to supply missing body language in un-bodied informal conversation. Written language has a more complex, more localized set of rules for civility. Where the substitutes for body language are scanty, unagreed or cross-cultural (as in online communications of various kinds) we have the greatest conversational hazards and the fewest safeguards against inhuman cruelty.

This isn't just playing about with words. The word 'conversation' describes mutually successful communication: it can also mean the sexual act. 'With thee conversing I forget all time,' says unfallen Eve to Adam in *Paradise Lost*[3] as they prepare to retire to their marriage bower; and sexual transgression has been legally described as 'criminal conversation'. The etymology of 'conversation' itself refers neither to language nor to touch, but to mutuality. It is a turn-and-turn-about word, a dancing-together word; it means paying attention to one another. It is a sign of dynamic order. And in this area, within the Church as outside it, we have exactly this problem: we aren't paying attention. Something halts our understanding.

---

2 Acts 2.1–13.

3 John Milton, *Paradise Lost*, IV.639, in *The Poetical Works of John Milton*, ed. Helen Darbishire (London: Oxford University Press, 1958), p. 89.

In the world in general there are lots of fractures in cultural communication – I will tangle with some of them later. But within the Church there are two particular communication issues. We don't agree about how God speaks through the Scriptures. And we don't agree about how the Scriptures speak into history. So I need to set out as lucidly as I can what I think happens when we read Scripture. Perhaps that might make it more possible to have a real Christian 'conversation' on the topic of holiness and desire.

Scripture and its work in time

Every day, several times a day, within my own Christian community, I read or hear passages of Scripture: from the Old Testament (the sacred writings of Judaism that were Jesus' inheritance) and from the New (the writings clustering around Jesus himself and his earliest followers). In certain ritual contexts, I will respond by affirming that I have heard God's voice speak. I do this in good faith.

This even though the Bible I receive is made up of a wider range of potentially sacred writings and its selection fixed through debate and discussion running between the second and the fourth century AD. This even though I know that the writings themselves are edited together from other, often lost texts, with multiple authors and a complex history of transmission and reception. That the names attached to particular books and sections are not stably identified with one named author but may have multiple or anonymous hands. That the 'scriptures' to which New Testament documents refer do not include any of the New Testament itself. How can I think God speaks in all this? To what am I assenting?

Yet I do assent. I assent because I think that the texts speak and live authoritatively within the Now of my engagement with them. I assent because my acceptance of the Scriptures as holy is not individual but collective and trans-historical. I accept the authority that requires me to take that selection and that reception history on trust. I will treat the letters of Paul and the other letters of the early Christian communities included in the

New Testament on a different footing from the collection of early teachings we call the *Didache*. I will treat the four canonical Gospels on a different footing from the apocryphal *Gospel of Thomas*. As a Christian I will take 'I know that my Redeemer lives', enigmatic words written in one of the oldest and most textually corrupt sections of the book of Job,[4] to be a prophetic declaration of the redeeming power of Jesus Christ; I will be reading the Jewish Scriptures from a very particular Christian angle. Textual history is not the last word for meaning.

I believe this is a necessary foundation for faith. It is deeply related to the part of me that believes stable communication is possible at all. Trusting the Scriptures is not wilful blindness but a speaking act of love. Because of love I believe that the power of a medieval anonymous lyric to move me to tears signals an authentic rather than a historically naive response. Because of love I believe that a paradisal early memory of playing with my brother upon a carpet of cherry blossom is a present earnest of the joys of heaven, not a corrupted image of a lost event. The fount of all these is the same as the belief that turns me towards my spouse trustfully rather than in suspicion.

As with my spouse, I pursue my relationship with Scripture assuming that the process of *becoming* that led to this communicative moment will, in the end, fulfil and not betray my trust. Not because it is a history of perfection – that's true neither of writing nor of people – but because love underpins the conversation, love makes it possible. Like all relationships it will have appalling, jagged gaps, breakdowns that seem insuperable. I will sometimes argue with it, sometimes be angry, sometimes disagree. That is how conversation is. For Scripture its crucible of meaning is the receiving intelligence, history, body and affections of the reader. Scripture makes itself vulnerable to my flaws and to my failures of understanding; the trust goes both ways. I am not expected to be 'mute and spiritless'[5] before its holy voice. But I must know how to listen.

---

4 Job 19.25.

5 John Milton said this of silent wives in *The Doctrine and Discipline of Divorce* (1642).

For the basis of my scriptural encounter, like the basis of my marriage, is not the disagreement, or the failures, but the trust. When I accept the Bible's unfolding identity I am saying that God acts in the accidental patterns of history, in its conflicts and mistakes as well as in its deliberate achievements. I don't need to know for sure that the author of the letter to the Colossians was Paul, only that he was listening to God. I am already reading by faith and not merely by sight. I am also assuming that the very mixed history of biblical interpretation is part of the raw material God transforms in redemptive power. This faith is like the faith that the mess I have made of some of my own relationships is transformed for good somehow by God's quick intervention. It's just on a much larger scale.

In the Anglican Church, we have another division of outlook. We *worship* with Scripture using poetic, symbolic ways of understanding, derived from interpretative work done by influential Church Fathers in the first few centuries after Christ. But we *reason* with it in a very different way, derived from arguments made by theologians at the Reformation who saw the biblical text as much more linear and transparent. So we have a huge communication gap between our worship and our reasoning. In worship we don't talk much about how to believe in poetic connections. And we divorce our reasoning from our corporate worshipping life, and so from our communal heart.

When we reason at arm's length with inert lumps of text, we cannot recognize how they and we communicate. Scripture in worship comes into the unfolding history of Now, binding together those who take part and making it more likely that they will take care with fragile shared meanings. Worship is recognized as a form of encounter. Enacted words are pregnant with change.

Often discussions of the Bible's authority seem to make distinctions between an atemporal, anti-historical vision which believes the Bible to be revelatory and a historical one which is much more doubtful. I think it is the other way round. I think that reading the Bible as a completely transparent single document refuses to trust God's readiness to act through the strange accidents of history. Such readers must fend off history in order to stay faithful. They are stuck at that early point in a marriage where any acceptance of flaw or finitude in a spouse will bring the whole edifice crashing down – a very vulnerable state. But it is a position of faith to read God's redemptive presence into the shifting patterns and disruptions of chance, violence and sin. Truth, by God's mercy, can be the miraculous daughter of Time. Meaning unfolds; it discloses itself through what has been and grows into what will arise, illuminated by the Christ who submitted himself to the depredations of time and yet is the same yesterday, today and for ever.

Through the words of the Scriptures God helps us understand his will and meaning across time and culture and human limitation; but the mediating filters of time, culture and human limitation, translatory though they are, are not God. The problem with scriptural authority is not a problem with whether there's enough God in the text. It's not that way round. The problem is instead with how possible it has been for the immensity of God's self to have been shoehorned within the narrow limits of human understanding across the centuries. The Scriptures bulge and creak with the effort of holding God.

It is even more absurd to say that God speaks through the Scriptures than it is to say that God confined and emptied himself into becoming a human being during a particular period of time. Yet without the speaking, without the body, how can we know God's majesty? It is no accident that Jesus is called the Word. To believe the Bible to be authoritative you must believe that the human and the divine are deeply intimate – that partial seeing has something true to say. With Jesus, and with the Scriptures, we are seeing eternity finding a way to say something time might understand. In the Word, God opens a conversation where both partners – God and humanity – have a place to speak.

But. But I do believe the embodied Word, Jesus as Word, to be more reliable than words. To live out the faith that Jesus is alive is to accept that the life of Jesus, experientially acting here and now, presides over the limits of text. The being of God is independent of historical cultural assumptions and pressures, independent of the unexamined prejudices of a time and an age, independent – come to that – of the unexamined prejudices of our own readings. The Bible is a container, and God cannot be contained. What it holds includes our act of trust in it, which is a significant – though not a decisive – part of what makes it the best we have, so far as artefacts go. But it is still an artefact.

Violence and intimacy in scriptural reading

Scripture has power. It has power for lots of reasons, but the big one is because God speaks through it. 'The word of God is living and active,' writes the author of the letter to the Hebrews, 'piercing until it divides soul from spirit, joints from marrow'.[6] But in Scripture we do not only meet God. We also meet human limits. Scripture is the divine and the human mixed up together.

We don't have any good method for picking the divine and the human apart. What would be grounds for it? Do we say God only speaks in the oldest parts – and why would that make sense? Or only in the parts where we can assign a certain human author? Why would that matter? Or in the parts where the manuscripts are most stable? So can God never work through chance? And since God always speaks into the blindness and greed of human history, we have to live somehow with knowing that even in Scripture purity is simply not available. We are pointed towards it, allowed a glimpse of it, visited by it – but it sits within the mess of everything else. A lot of Scripture simply describes the mess. Cherry-picking for the bits we can stand to hear is a kind of cheating.

The meeting of human and divine in a mortal container is the heart of Christian belief. We can trust that Scripture shows us truth through, as well as in spite of, its limitations. God is allowing himself to be vulnerable to the misreadings of the human/divine mix by manifesting at all – just as Jesus made himself vulnerable to the 'readings' both of individuals in desperate need and of a murderously angry crowd.

---

6 Hebrews 4.12.

Jesus' conception and birth made humanity holy. Was there anything of Mary in Christ? In the oldest layer of incarnational theology the ancient medical belief that a mother is nothing but an incubator simplified the answer; but they were wrong. The *theotokos*, the God-carrier, gives her shape and substance to what is carried. So even the flawedness of the humanity in Scripture shapes the nature of its divine insight for good.

This means that the way we read Scripture is unique. We can't ourselves understand where soul parts from spirit or joints from marrow, because these things are parts of a whole. The images seem to be chosen for their indivisibility – will the word of God separate us from our essential selves? Why would that be a good thing? Except for one thing – the nature of the incarnate Word himself – we might seem to be left without defence in this mixed scriptural presence, a field for irrigation, harrowing, planting, watering, scything.

As the rain and the snow come down from heaven,
and do not return there until they have watered the earth;
making it bring forth and sprout,
giving seed to the sower and bread to the eater:
so shall my word be that goes out from my mouth;
it shall not return to me empty,
but it shall accomplish that which I purpose,
and succeed in the things for which I sent it.

So says the Lord through the medium of the third writer to be called 'Isaiah' in the book of that name (Isaiah 55.10–11). This is a benign image of fruitful change, but look how powerless it seems to make us. If God is our world and our weather, our seasons his times, our soil his field, what choice have we about the effect of the word we hear? Between life or death, destruction or making new, the choice appears to be in the world and the weather, not the soil. In such an image the voice of God is irresistible.[7]

---

7 The song 'Love Rain' by the poet and singer Jill Scott re-purposes the images of this Isaiah passage for talking about human passion and betrayal to dramatic and unsettling effect. It is on *Who is Jill Scott?* (1999).

Or that's what a violent model of scriptural reading would say. The violent model notices how impossible it is to separate human and divine, and 'solves' the problem by announcing everything about the text to be divine. The human reader becomes passive and abject, a blank to be filled. There is no place for the work of understanding; no space to rise to meet thoughts and images with personal memory or imagination or judgement. I do not believe that this kind of power is truly the power of the Word. When a reader is reduced to passivity, it will not be God's power that crushes her. Mixed in with the voice of God, and impossible to disentangle from it, will be the cultural, linguistic and conceptual scaffolding of Scripture's framers and containers – by which I mean both those of the original writers and the fears and assumptions of the reader herself.

For this is a terrifying way to understand holy reading. How can the conversational voices between self and Scripture ever be true partners? How will we know whether what we hear is mortal container or the divine it contains? Is that even a meaningful distinction? Yet – since we *can't* distinguish – is this model perhaps the only model open to us? If so, then how are we to stay separate, choosing, assenting beings when we are laid so constantly open to heavenly change? Does, in other words, the worship of God *require* the worship of Scripture? Is reading Scripture really a form of intimate violence?

I don't believe it is. I don't think intimate violence is right for Scripture, any more than for any other relationship. (It is not the relationship model described in Ephesians 5.28.) I don't believe that God wills the use of his irresistible power to set impossible conditions for his human readers. Quite the reverse. God is good. Because Jesus was born, the earth that makes us up is also powerfully holy. Our mortality shines with God's presence. Soil affects seed. 'Prosper thou the works of our hands', writes the psalmist at the end of one of the great psalms on death, Psalm 90.[8] Even our mistakes may be changed into glory: it is called *redemption*. God is careful to approach us, in Scripture as in prayer, as conversation partners. We are not

---

8 Psalm 90.17, Book of Common Prayer.

rushed or shouted into assent. God always and everywhere saves us from himself, even when it means that bad things will happen through human folly. Jesus his Son, in the days of his flesh and now in the days of the Spirit, asks us what we want of him.[9] God invites, converses, waits. He asked Abraham.[10] He asked Moses.[11] He asked Mary.[12] He asks us. His cloud is a veil; it is not the dark housing for a thunderbolt. He keeps himself hidden enough to ensure our freedom; he does not even seduce, let alone override, the will.

It is a very ancient metaphor that we are defenceless women to God's masculine force. John Donne, from the confining fortress of his own masculinity, was charmed by it:

Take me to you, imprison me, for I
Except you enthrall me, never shall be free
Nor ever chaste, except you ravish me.[13]

But we can be sure that Donne did not get what he asked for. God does not ravish, even when we long to be forced away from our own worst choices; even when other things in the world are less honourable in the ways they wield their weapons – addictions and temptations and greed. Still God remains quiet, as his Son Jesus remained silent before his ac-cusers when they held the power of life and death over him. He makes himself always more vulnerable than we could ever ask or imagine in hiding his power. He speaks not in earthquake, wind or fire but in the *batqol* – the 'daughter of a voice'.[14] In

---

9 Mark 10.51; Luke 18.41; Luke 24.28–29; John 1.38; John 5.6; John 6.5b; John 8.10; John 11.26; John 21.15–19; Acts 8.26–39; Acts 9.4.

10 Genesis 15.

11 Exodus 3.11–12.

12 Luke 1.26–38.

13 John Donne, Holy Sonnet 10, in *The Oxford Authors: John Donne*, ed. John Carey (Oxford: Oxford University Press, 1990), pp. 177–8.

14 1 Kings 19.11–12. The word *batqol* is translated, variously, as 'a still small voice' and 'a thread of a voice' and (wittily) 'the sound of sheer silence'.

the sound of his sheer silence, if we pay attention to it, we find freedom to speak.[15] Next time you chide God for saying nothing, thank him at the same time for his restraint.

Scripture as conversation

Scripture is vulnerable to what its readers bring to it. We who read help to make meaning and we are not God. To live is to change continually; and Scripture lives. When God chooses to inhabit written meaning, he becomes vulnerable, confined in a frail time-limited body and exposed to the prejudices, fears and other baggage of those who approach him. That baggage also has power to transform, and not always in a good way. What we bring colours what we find. Reading can be a kind of mirror from which strange nightmare faces peer. For a woman reading, the experience can be one like sexual violence; for someone else with a different history or context the terrors of judgement, punishment or abandonment may be more present. 'Even from my youth up thy terrors have I suffered with a troubled mind,' writes the psalmist.[16]

The seventeenth-century devotional writer John Bunyan (who deeply influenced the spiritual shaping of modern Anglo-American culture) talked about the Word that would 'fall like an hot thunderbolt . . . on my conscience'.[17] For Bunyan, anxious Calvinist, scrutinizing the text intensely for signs that he

---

15 I don't propose, incidentally, to discuss pronouns and God, except to say that this is the reason why I cling to the (inadequate, incomplete) masculine pronoun for God for much of the time – the only 'He' in my experience unafraid of silence, complete in vulnerability, absolute for a defenceless love. I do not, however, think that there is something essentially masculine about the creator of all, and recognize that the default use of the masculine fits ill with the gender anxiety of pronoun use that dominates all modern discourse.

16 Psalm 88.15b, Book of Common Prayer.

17 John Bunyan, *Grace Abounding to the Chief of Sinners* (London, 1666), para 163 (Project Gutenberg), www.gutenberg.org/files/654/654-h/ 654-h.htm (accessed 09.01.2020).

might be saved or damned, the Word acted upon the reader. He suffered before Scripture daily. His spiritual autobiography, *Grace Abounding to the Chief of Sinners*, describes the cycle of suffering in agonizing detail. His journey towards understanding the Word as a place of life and health was long and winding. His sense of himself as alienated from God's goodness meant that he did not expect to find the Spirit of truth already within him.

He learnt that he was wrong. God's covenant is 'I AM with you'. The incarnation shows God in human knowing, feeling and being. We are not made up only of nightmare voices; we are also made to ring true. 'This commandment that I am commanding you today is not too hard for you', says the Lord, 'nor is it too far away. It is not in heaven, that you should say, "Who will go up into heaven for us, and get it for us so that we may hear it and observe it?" . . . No, the word is very near to you; it is in your mouth and in your heart for you to observe.'[18] Readers participate in the intimate divine encounter; this is just as true when we meet God in the Scriptures as it was for those who met Jesus on the road. In the Spirit's presence, time loses its power. 'Were not our hearts burning within us', exclaim the two on the way to Emmaus, 'while he was talking to us on the road, while he was opening the scriptures to us?'[19] With thee conversing I forget all time.

Bunyan had a biblical source for his image of a 'Word' that fell upon him, but in its source it brought blessing, not punishment. There is a moment in the Acts of the Apostles where a group of non-Jewish men receive the Spirit on hearing the testimony of Peter: 'the Holy Spirit fell upon all who heard the word'.[20] The Word fell into lived experience. For the Gentiles of Caesarea, that Word fell *outside* the Scriptures, as a speech-experience; it became transformatory baptism in spite of the limitations of those Scriptures as they then existed. The whole chapter (Acts 10) shows Peter, the faithful Jew, learning that the word of God

---

18 Deuteronomy 30.11–14.
19 Luke 24.32.
20 Acts 10.44.

frees itself from what is already written, as Jesus is freed from the tomb; and even before Peter has finished speaking the Spirit completes his thought in what happens next. 'Can anyone withhold the water for baptizing these people . . . ?' asks Peter. His Jewish companions gaze upon the power descended from above and assent to the Gentiles' full and proper place in the Christian family. Everyone is attending to what God is doing in front of them as well as to what they read. When we read, we are mixing our present-world experience with God's divine change.

Embodying Scripture

Can the textual Word act in the world? Modern readers instinctively think of the written word as dis-embodied – protean, ephemeral, edgeless yet without depth, as flat as the screens we scan and skip for 'content'. If knowledge is Isaac Newton's sea, we are more likely to be skimming the stones we find on the beach over it than bothering to examine them for what they might tell us; and we are astonishingly indifferent to the depths over which we make them bounce. We seldom speak what we read; much of what happens with reading is happening inside people's heads much faster than events in real time.

Reading can leave the body behind – the internal self forgets its flesh. The principle of the imagined avatar in online gaming is based on such forgetting. In the imaginary world we are more apt to believe that meanings are fixed, unaffected by time and physicality. This is not true. The same words will speak differently into different times, events, people, places; the same person will understand a different truth in the same words read years apart. Our vision of text as unbodied betrays us, and the mistake is remarkably modern. People were much more likely to sound out words as they read a couple of hundred years ago, to learn things by heart. Words existed in lips and lungs and palates and breath as much as they existed in text. The young Florence Nightingale, furious in trapped rebellion as she searched for a way to pursue her nursing vocation, experienced someone reading aloud to her as assault:

What is it to be read aloud to? . . . It is like lying on one's back, with one's hands tied and having liquid poured down one's throat. Worse than that, because suffocation would immediately ensue and put a stop to the operation. But nothing would stop the other.[21]

It's a particularly striking image – reading as waterboarding – a precursor too of the force-feeding that suffragettes would experience a little more than half a century later. *That* was how powerful the spoken word was to her. Words spoken aloud, in time and space and company, make things happen.

We do not read aloud very much at all now – except in church. And too often we bring impoverished assumptions to it. Public reading can be sloppy, a verbal ratification of a text we've already got in writing; and as we listen we are busily shoving its words back into the flat page, and feeling impatiently that having to hear them in time from a human voice is slow. Yet these are texts written to be sounded. To be heard in time and in a particular – often communal and liturgical – context; to be dropped down into the depths of experience, to be pondered, drawn up, measured, dropped and raised again. A living reading will show as it tells, and isn't just about smoothly marking the grammatical turns.

In the last year I have received living Scripture several times. A man reading a Pauline epistle in church after a stroke, discovering phrase by phrase what he is being told. A teenage boy at Easter Eve visibly and dramatically astonished at the events of the Red Sea crossing, where reading became a fast, wild, choppy ride. A dramatically skilful reader bringing Nehemiah's dedication to rebuilding the Temple alive in Westminster Abbey. Scripture *can* speak through us. It is remarkable how seldom it is allowed to.

Before we were so used to throwaway text, in the days when we still had to memorize, we used to collect nuggets of meaning from Scripture and carry them around in our heads. They were

---

21 *Cassandra: An Essay by Florence Nightingale* (New York: The Feminist Press, 1979 [1852]), p. 34.

bits of found sea wrack, to be turned in the pocket and felt and held. Small and powerful, they spoke into daily experience more readily out of their own context. 'Vengeance is mine, saith the Lord.'[22] 'Do not let the sun go down on your anger.'[23] 'Though I walk through the valley of the shadow of death, yet thou art with me.'[24] 'Our mouth shall show forth thy praise.'[25] 'In my Father's house are many mansions.'[26] Becoming proverbial, they also helped people make decisions about how they lived.

Liturgy is full of Scripture behaving this way, as a nugget, or a graftable cutting, striking its foreign life into new ground. Sometimes the field of meaning from the old enriches its placement: 'O Lord, open our lips' gains enormously when you know it is the turn towards joy near the end of the penitential Psalm 51. Sometimes it does a different job – the original surround for 'Thy almighty Word leaped down from heaven',[27] words of incarnation, is strange and violent. Scripture can live as powerfully and as fruitfully outside linear meanings as within them.

There are other modes for embodied Scripture. Worship songs allow felt contemplation of phrases, passages, even single images: think how Matt Redman's hugely popular '10,000 Reasons' meditates on a phrase from Psalm 103: 'Bless the LORD, O my soul.' The practice of *lectio divina* (divine reading) moves away from analysis towards embodied attention. It cuts across the usual divide between 'Bible study' and liturgical participation. It is a discipline to hear a passage voiced by different readers. To sit with it in silence and pay attention to how the Word speaks then and there. To forbid yourself fancy explanations. A Scripture that changes its emphasis with the person and the time is a Word in conversation. It is alive.

---

22 Romans 12.19 (1611 translation), lightly paraphrased.
23 Ephesians 4.26.
24 Psalm 23.4 (1611 translation).
25 Matins and Evensong response from the Book of Common Prayer, adapted from a singular to a plural collective voice and quoting Psalm 51.15.
26 John 14.2 (1611 translation).
27 Wisdom 18.15–17 (1611 translation).

But risky. Scripture that speaks in time and space is vulnerable to mistake, misunderstanding, carelessness, to the loud refusals of defiance, or the silent disengagements of the abject, enslaved reader. These are not conversation. We cannot hear Scripture well without the Holy Spirit to direct and vivify the encounter. Intelligence is not enough. Some truths shine just for the moment and then retire; others live longer. Some kinds of approach are too alienated, and some are too self-absorbed. Relationships do not thrive in those conditions. Reading, in the kind of attention it asks for, is a form of prayer, as well as a form of love.

Scriptural encounter and the sexuality debates

The Church of England's sexuality debates, focused on same-sex relationships and gender identity, have been full of collisions. They cluster around different understandings of the power of Scripture as it acts in time. What weight are we supposed to give to original historical context, for example in the condemnation of same-sex practices in the often-discussed passage of Romans 1? If original context is granted a defining weight, is it there to be explained away, replaced by the morals of our own cultural context? Or is it there to challenge those morals? Or is history beside the point, a distraction from the eternal divine message? Supposing we *were* to grant history ultimate power, would we (for example) ditch New Testament passages influenced by obsolete views of the cosmos and its hierarchy of spiritual powers? Where does it stop?

While I don't accept the static reading that bows before every scriptural sentence (and I've never met anyone who has managed to do this with *every* scriptural sentence) I don't think 'original context' can have the last word. The text has continued to live and breathe – and, yes, change in what it needs to tell us – over the millennia from then to now. In Scripture as in literature, theatre or music, we do not learn as much as you might think by reconstructing your best guess at its earliest surround. You can't really revive what it was like to be someone else long ago. The truth does not lie in past readings, though past readings inform it; the truth lies in the interactive work the words are doing with us as we meet them. And what the words are doing now will sit uneasily with the mixed mess of original context, so that we need the guidance of the Spirit, who assists us to read conversationally, who guides our sense of right doing and being, to know what is superseded.

Christ has been working in the world for a long time now, outside as well as inside the textual frame, in the actions of holiness, the gradual shifts in what we understand humanity to be. When we try to understand the nature of divorce, or of the role of women, or the nature of committed sexual relationships, we might be like Peter dreaming of what is free to eat, or Paul discovering that the Spirit falls upon the Gentiles. The Word breaks out of its textual confines all the time. But we need to know that our dreams are not merely generated by the heat of our own desires.

Though biblical writings are very various, they all show – in one way or another – God intervening into particular lives, places, times and people now thousands of years old. And they *are* particular. Few bits of the Bible offer fortune-cookie generality, stuff that can be slapped on to any human situation. Find an 'inspiring' bit, just about anywhere you open the book, and a second later some disconcerting – and at times violent – shift of perspective will trip you up. Often the piece of Scripture you find will undermine some previous religious code, show the presence of God in an unexpected place. Following rigid behavioural rules as a way to salvation is undermined within the Scriptures about as often as it is recommended.

And, almost everywhere, our interpretations have to use some form of symbolic translation for them to make any kind of sense. Even finding prophetic traces of the subsequent history of the Church, or the nature of the Trinity, or the Church's historic but post-biblical institutional practices (like ordination) takes selective ingenuity, much of it now very old and therefore accepted, just as Christians accept reading of the Old Testament in the light of the New.

How much Christ is foreshadowed in the Old Testament is only the most central of the interpretative decisions we inherit in a project that ties together wild divergence. Usually it does this through a mixture of typology (linking different historical events by identifying them as participating in the same nugget of shared story or powerful character) and synecdoche (reading out from the naming of a part of something the significance of the whole). Noah's flood as a foreshadowing of Christian baptism. The rejection of an obscure steward in Isaiah 22 with the rejection of Judas Iscariot as a disciple. The Jordan as the river through which we pass from death to life. Zion as the city of heaven. What lambs mean, or grains of wheat, or loaves of bread, or vines, or shepherds, kings, temples, wilderness. The nature of the word 'Spirit' or the changing character, reach and ambition of God (he seems, in the beginning, only to be locally interested yet by the end his engagement is universal), or the particularity of sin and its shifting relationship to cultural impurity. The Bible is all about change.

If we forget these things, if we forget the breathing, speaking body that is Scripture and treat it as an inert lump, we run the risk of using it to construct an axe or a spear, a slingstone or a tombstone – or to contemplate the peculiar pleasures of pressing each other to death. And this is particularly true when we are asking Scripture to serve as ammunition in a debate over behaviour, over whether a change is a good change or self-serving.

But conversation is not debate. A conversation needs to be very attentive to arguments that cheat or trap the listener. A conversation always has to hold open the possibility, on every side, of *metanoia*, of changing your mind. God himself – so Scripture tells us – consented in conversation to have his mind changed.[28]

Reading is always relational. In that case, our care in reading needs to be like our care in all other relationships. The rules are not different.

---

28 Genesis 18.17–end; Exodus 32.7–14; Mark 7.24–30; Matthew 15.21–28.

The conventions and behaviours of sexual desire have altered so fast in my lifetime that I have been forced, sometimes through my own contradictory, confused and at times disastrous responses and decisions, to notice how quickly moral consensus changes. I may be of the last generation to have been routinely invited to take Scripture seriously. The chances of my life and its time have taken me across a huge cultural fault line, watching and participating in the traumatic process of cultural change. I am someone whose angle of vision is almost accidentally – or providentially – useful. And because the encounter between lived experience and Scripture is where I believe the conversation to be located, this book appeals to personal experience and to different cultural voices, as well as speaking with and to the scriptural voice. It's a risky method, and it allows plenty of space to disagree. But, then, that's conversation.

PART 2

Desire

*Which is about human desire in modern life,
and what happens to our longing for more than we can
immediately see, touch or buy.*

2

Longing

Longing as meaning

In a recent album, *Darkness and Light*, the singer-songwriter John Legend wonders aloud how his baby daughter will fare growing up into the world he knows, a world 'run by desire'.[1]

I do not believe that the vitality of desire is humankind's main problem. Quite the reverse. I don't think that our spiritual energies should be engaged upon the lifelong, doomed task of evading, banishing, neutralizing or – failing all else – finding ways to slip out temporarily from under its power. We, good stoics, would lose in our achieved indifference . . . *all this*: longing, wanting, lacking, yearning, wishing, hoping, burning, hungering, thirsting, calling, praying, reaching, remembering, mourning. Without these the only thing left to want is death.

'Ah, but a man's reach should exceed his grasp,' wrote Robert Browning, 'Or what's a heaven for?'[2] But does heaven have to be 'for' anything? And – if heaven must be useful – who makes it so? The question acknowledges that the idea of 'heaven' may be powerful, even necessary, but that it might not be true. It could be a fantasy, constructed only to keep longing alive. In the context of the poem, it sounds almost like a counsel of despair.

Browning's lines escaped their context and became an inspirational aphorism about the ambitious scope of human

---

1 John Legend, 'Right by You (for Luna)', on *Darkness and Light* (2016).

2 Robert Browning, 'Andrea del Sarto', in *Men and Women* (1855).

perception. On their own, the lines keep God at a controllable distance, allowing for a 'vision' with a human centre that can drip into itself optional homeopathic doses of the divine as a brightener. They stand quite neatly for a family of inspirational tropes that animate the 'vision' (or 'mission') of most commercial enterprises, ennobling business with faintly spiritualized human endeavour.

Yet others have seen the aphorism's complex undertones. R. H. Tawney, in his influential book *Religion and the Rise of Capitalism*, writes, 'Men are to be judged by their reach as well as by their grasp.'[3] He means that in spite of the gulf fixed between the social good humankind might envision and its actual capacity to make good things happen, it is urgently necessary to honour and pursue the good. While he does not ask what heaven is for, his whole book could be considered as measuring the heaven we pray for in 'thy kingdom come' against the narrative of European religious and economic history up to World War Two. Tawney influenced Archbishop William Temple profoundly in his articulation of a practical social gospel.[4] In our own century, the thrust of Justin Welby's publishing and campaigning history as Archbishop of Canterbury attaches itself deliberately to the same perception, with the same emphasis on the importance of civic and national hope.[5]

Modern culture is in the business of narrowing the distance between 'reach' and 'grasp', in a project designed to make 'heaven' unnecessary. (Heaven really is a place on earth.[6]) Rhetoric about the ambition of the human spirit is built into

---

3 R. H. Tawney, 'Conclusion' to *Religion and the Rise of Capitalism* (London: John Murray, 1926), p. 301.

4 William Temple, *Christianity and Social Order* (London: Penguin, 1942).

5 See Justin Welby, *Reimagining Britain: Foundations for Hope* (London: Bloomsbury, 2018).

6 'Heaven is a Place on Earth' is an enduringly popular power ballad, sung by Belinda Carlisle in 1987 but still going strong, with a recent anime revival.

commerce, into civic rhetoric, into education. When 'reach' and 'grasp' are treated as synonyms, possibility and fulfilment can be made to melt improbably into each other. The promise of fulfilment is everywhere, from the can-do HSBC adverts that line the walls of airport jet bridges to the words of the secular primary school song 'Believe',[7] which carelessly loads on to every child the burden of compulsory success: asking them to sing about being able to do anything – climb mountains, navigate oceans, 'anything at all' – if they can just believe in themselves.

This is a great positioning for advertising. Adverts exploit the gap between hope and fulfilment by implying that the one will become the other. Adverts also need them not to, because fulfilment doesn't sell things. In watching an advert we are watching a fantasy from which our sophisticated distance is assumed. Adverts are constructed to exert influence rather than to command assent, though the less sophisticated rollover that assent delivers is always welcome.

Yet the gap between hope and fulfilment that adverts pretend to bridge is a gap we need. Fulfilment that extinguishes hope renders its own benefits invisible. The gap is where we live, the place of desire. And when the gap is only acknowledged with success as a precondition ('with this hope to drive me onward', as Marsh's song optimistically puts it) desire is dangerously harnessed. For those many – those most; those all – who discover that the mountains are, after all, too high, the ocean too dangerously wild and wet and deep, failure and shame attend an astonished disappointment. Nothing to wish for except the thing we failed at, nothing to hope for except the thing we thought was already our due. Nothing acknowledged to be beyond the human grasp. Success might even be worse – no bounds, no checks, no perspective. If the whole universe is imagined to be smaller than a single human will, then that single human will is a giant adrift in a wilderness of nowhere. But we are not giants. We are small people tricking ourselves.

---

7 Lin Marsh, 'Believe' (2005).

We are confined in ways that the songs and the adverts simply will not admit.

'What's a heaven for?'

You can only sing 'imagine there's no heaven' with real enthusiasm if you truly believe that there's an easily closable gap between reach and grasp. The lyrics of John Lennon's song are millenarian, eschatological. 'I saw no temple in the city,' writes the visionary: the perfect time when humankind sings in harmony and lives in peace is virtually here – or just around the corner, anyway.[8] But it wasn't. It isn't. In the end, the longing of a song like 'Imagine' is exactly the same as the longing for heaven in Browning's poem – it points to a wonderful elsewhere that cannot be touched. As I was growing up, across the 1970s and 1980s, people seemed uncertain about whether it couldn't be touched because it had already happened (the 1960s being so decisively over, so enviable) or whether it was on its way somehow and still unfolding.

The headmaster of my primary school preached to us almost weekly about the imminent coming of the end-times, newspaper in hand to match current events up to the relevant passages from Revelation. We would all sing 'God is working his purpose out', accompanied by wailing recorders. 'And the earth shall be filled with the glory of God as the waters cover the sea.' I became wary of apocalyptic sunsets. I prayed that Christ would not come in my lifetime, or my children's, or my children's children's, on and on as far as I could imagine my intercessory intervention running. I wasn't sure it was going to work.

---

8 Revelation 21.22. See also Sam Brewitt-Taylor for the church version of this expectation, in *Christian Radicalism in the Church of England and the Invention of the British Sixties, 1957–1970* (Oxford: Oxford University Press, 2018).

Once John Lennon was shot, in 1980, it became clear that heaven was not round the corner at all: it had been and gone. The world was back to its sordid business-as-usual. The boyfriends I went out with (some of them) yelled along to Crass's anti-nuclear blast: 'They've got a bomb.'[9] Personally, I was bored and alienated by punk, so loud, local and masculine (Hersham was four stops away, its boys a nuisance at parties[10]), took refuge in the last gasps of romantic, space-age eschatology, buying my stairways to heaven with (Tim) Blake's *New Jerusalem*, King Crimson's *Islands* with its astonishing cover of stars, Led Zeppelin's 'Battle of Evermore', or even the more terrestrial wistfulness of 'Going to California'.[11] I tried not to notice the ways they were absurd or downright repulsive, or the boredom of long improvisations, or how necessary it was to be a man to enter prog rock paradise. I tried to play the piano like Keith Emerson,[12] but only managed to be nicknamed after the piano-playing dog on *The Muppet Show*. I didn't want to think heaven could never arrive, though I had my fair share of four-minute-warning dreams. I asked my mother, in 1979, whether she was afraid. 'Not after Cuba,' she said.

Deus and deixis[13]

So what's a heaven for? It is the place of desire; and we reach towards it through the passions of experience.

---

9 Crass, 'They've got a Bomb', on *Stations of the Cross* (1978).

10 'Hersham Boys', a single released by the punk rock band Sham 69, reached number 6 in the charts in 1979. Hersham is a commuter town on the southern main line from London.

11 Tim Blake, *Blake's New Jerusalem* (1978), King Crimson, *Islands* (1971), *Led Zeppelin IV* (1971).

12 Keith Emerson was a classically trained virtuoso keyboardist best known for his Hammond Organ playing in the 1960s band The Nice and his synthesizer work in the 1970s supergroup Emerson, Lake and Palmer. See https://en.wikipedia.org/wiki/Keith_Emerson (accessed 08.01.2020).

13 'Deixis' is the technical term for words dependent upon the context of time and/or place for how they are read; so that although their meaning remains stable where they point relies on situation. For example, pronouns, or denotations of place or time such as here, there, then.

Our delight in the present and tangible is not confined inside a point called now. It spreads out from it, backwards and forwards through time. It connects the immediate (now) to the unattainable (then). It does this in the associations of memory, which is the form for longing after what once was. And it does this also in the way that we look, in a strangely similar longing, towards what has not yet come to be, the sight just at the edge of our vision. The experience of becoming, of being someone who has an unfolding meaning in the world, is absolutely dependent upon experience we can't possess, experience lent to us through imagination and in memory. Somewhere over the rainbow waits the living fulfilment of all our longing: I AM, the God who simply and always is, the God in whom our own being finds what we were ever there for. My Christian faith trusts desire to contain all meaning; in desire my eyeline lifts up beyond what is available, pressing forward towards something I am too small to possess. While we are creatures who value yearning, who know that our reach exceeds our grasp, we are able also to be creatures looking beyond the visible towards what we cannot yet see or touch, towards the mystery of things. Desire keeps the future open and the past breathing; it invests the present with potential, a charge of power it cannot retain by itself.

The immediate is important. But alone it is vulnerable to despair. Desire invests the immediate and the tangible with potential, so that every experience becomes bigger than its own moment. Desire is our bridge out of the rule of time; and even if that bridge is barred presently by the toll gates of marketing campaigns it is still possible to find ways to look into a priceless distance. 'Buy wine and milk without money and without price,' invites God through the poetry of the third writer to be called Isaiah. 'Why do you spend your money for that which is not bread, and your labour for that which does not satisfy?'[14]

This is the way that Christians live out their yearning to abide with God, encountering him, tangible and knowable in being human, as Jesus was tangible and knowable in his humanity,

---

14 Isaiah 55.1b–2a.

yet at the same time longed for in a continuing absence because Jesus has gone before us and dwells with God beyond these human limits. We wait for his coming again, looking up and out, looking beyond ourselves, looking for signs of his presence in the faces and bodies and stories that surround us in the here and now. Across the New Testament, *now* and *not yet* dance together. What is faith? asks the writer of the letter to the Hebrews; and answers with a paradox, 'the substance of things hoped for, the evidence of things not seen'.[15] 'Hope does not disappoint,' writes St Paul.[16] The tension of presence with absence, hope with recognition written across the epistles rings true to me. 'Beloved, we are God's children now; what we will be has not yet been revealed. What we do know is this: when he is revealed, we will be like him, for we will see him as he is.'[17] Like the psalmist and the lover, the Christian dreams about what it might be like to wake up. Without hope – without its freight of desire – everything we already possess loses weight and value. When we behave as if the New Jerusalem is already here, we are bound for disappointment.

The heart-changing stories of humanity's desire are not about careless delight or tearless potency. Ours is not a Captain Marvel story. We do not have to imagine what it is like to possess bodies impervious to violence or age, or minds indifferent to the passing of time. Our narratives of seeking and finding end not in strangeness but in recognition. For Christians, God manifests in the known human face, in the weakness of a baby, the rare vulnerability of an unarmed man, the defencelessness of offered love, the keeping company with a dying body, the un-looked-for meeting seen through passionate tears. God inhabits the everyday truths of weakness, finitude and loss. The story of Jesus invests every lived moment with the holiness of God, because the Christian God lives and has died in time. So we are constantly infused with God's breathing presence – and perhaps so reliant upon it that we take no care to notice or

---

15 Hebrews 11.1, in the King James translation of 1611.
16 Romans 5.5.
17 1 John 3.2.

enjoy its gifts. Yet our souls wither when – whether in satiation or in starvation – we cease to pay attention to hope. 'Possibility is neither forever nor instant. It is not easy to sustain belief in its efficacy,' writes the poet Audre Lord.[18]

For what God is, spreads out into what was, and into what will be, tying everything to everything else in longing, in desire, in hope, in love. There is no place without God; infusing *now*, and *then*, and *there*, and *here*, with the meaning of story and pattern and selfhood. Because of Jesus, God's presence is strong in the places where the human imagination quails or retreats – with the degraded, the despairing, the imprisoned, the raped, the assimilated or devoured, those of damaged or vanished memory, the dying, those in pain, the tortured and humiliated, those in social exile. All the places that bring human sympathy to a standstill, that darken human comprehension, unreeling the heart towards meaninglessness – those are the places God inhabits with special care. There are no locked doors in the divine imagination. This is a very great mercy of its own, because the burdens of human suffering and human cruelty are too heavy to bear without despair or the wish for annihilation. Live in the place of death for long enough and death is what you will long for. But another heart helps bear that burden and another eye looks when we cannot, opening a door out of the dark confines of earth and dust.

> Where can I go then from your spirit? Or where can I flee from your presence?
> If I climb up to heaven, you are there; if I make the grave my bed, you are there also.
> If I take the wings of the morning and dwell in the uttermost parts of the sea,
> Even there your hand shall lead me, your right hand hold me fast.[19]

---

18 Audre Lord, 'Poetry is not a Luxury', in *The Master's Tools will never Dismantle the Master's House* (talk first given and then published in 1977 in *Chrysalis: A Magazine of Female Culture*).
19 Psalm 139.6–9, *Common Worship* translation.

Paradise is a place of mercy and restoration, where tears are wiped away rather than where they were never shed. 'Weeping may endure for a night, but joy cometh in the morning.'[20]

'Run by desire'

So, then, what's wrong with a world 'run by desire'? If it is the ultimate good thing, the bridge to eternity, the raw material of meaning, the life-motor? What's not to like? But turn the thought around. This isn't about a world unexpectedly illuminated by wild desire, but one with its wildness trapped into serving short-term, deliberately short-lived pleasures. And our world, the world of the modern West, though it cannot trap all the wild desire there is, has managed to enslave desire on a truly industrial, truly global scale.

I do not know exactly what John Legend means as he sings to his baby. But the potential of a new baby is one of the very few places where our vision is long; where we clearly understand desire to be about a relationship between the immediate present and a possibly wonderful future. Babies require patience. They don't always oblige with smiles and cute moments. You can't rely on what you'll get looking after a baby – though it will be unexpectedly wonderful at odd moments. Caring for babies means a grinding and monotonous set of vital, continual mini-tasks; it is as different as it possibly can be from the harnessing of desire for swift gratification.

There is little space for the needs of babies – or wildlife, or insects, or trees or oceans or glaciers – in a world run by desire. Desire as a motor for immediate reward drives towards possession rather than care, possessions rather than relationships. It is harnessed in order to direct and distract us only towards objects we can completely encompass. It encourages us to think about non-human stuff – whether we mean by that the 27,000 miles of submerged mountain ranges at the bottom of the sea

---

20 Psalm 30.5b, Book of Common Prayer. The overall point is much more eloquently made in W. H. Auden's poem 'Homage to Clio' (1960).

or our distance from the indifferent stars – as items that at least metaphorically can be 'handled', owned in the hand. What does it say about the human relationship with the wilds of space that a businessman might send up a Tesla car to orbit one of its stars?[21] (And even that has its own *joie de vivre* – unlike the many car adverts that fetishize the solitary landscapes the car economy continues to endanger and across which, on our crowded roads, no car driver may travel alone.) Yet to have and to hold means nothing without the stuff that we can't just have, can't quite grasp; the associations of the lost past; the potential of what might come; the wildness of what can't be understood. The wickedness of many car adverts is that (like certain kinds of global tourism) they pretend we can buy wildness.

In a world run, rather than filled, by desire, our grasp is so continual and so driven that we forget that we have any reach at all. We are under compulsion – a word meaning enslavement – flogging the moment to beat a residual grain of longing or memory out of its blankness, or killing the time watching a procession of the wonderfully alien artfully domesticated into small-screen cliché. 'It was no great mistake', remarks the seventeenth-century mystic Thomas Traherne, 'to say, that to have blessings and not to prize them is to be in Hell. For it maketh them ineffectual, as if they were absent. Yea, in some respects it is worse than to be in Hell. It is more vicious, and more irrational.'[22] Living becomes a crowded list of short-term goals and greeds. When we forget our reach we also forget our own small size; we forget that we shall die; we forget that we do not make ourselves, or live to ourselves, or die to ourselves.[23] We forget that there is anything bigger than the self. We spend our entire lives in the act of distracted forgetting to avert our own mortality. It is not being very good for us.

21 See www.telegraph.co.uk/news/2018/02/06/tech-giant-elon-musk-send-car-mars-aboard-worlds-powerful-rocket/ (accessed 08.01.2020).

22 Thomas Traherne, *Centuries of Meditations*, 47, in Thomas Traherne, *Centuries* (Leighton Buzzard: Clarendon Press, 1960), p. 23.

23 Romans 14.7.

Heart's desire

In 2016, The Who's early song 'The Seeker' (1970) became the music for a First Choice Holidays advert.[24] The advert goes like this. A pretty young woman is standing in a queue when she sees an ice-cream van go by with the words 'Heart's Desire' on the side. She seizes a bicycle and pedals eagerly after it. Coming to a handy lake, she dives in, her day-clothes float away and she emerges in stylish swimwear on an island paradise peopled with servilely handsome young men in pink. She searches for the perfect ice cream here, there and everywhere, enjoying the amenities of the island as she goes, pursued by sexual possibility and a gaggle of charming children who keep the mood moderately domestic. As the advert closes we see her choosing from an array of elaborate ice creams presented by beautiful men, and we can reasonably assume that the products they offer, like the famously rude Flake adverts of the 1960s onwards, are some kind of metaphor.

The Who's soundtrack song is about pursuing the meaning of life, originally written to express what its author Pete Townshend called 'Divine Desperation'.[25] But the advert has excised its punchline, where the singer predicts that he won't find what he is looking for except by dying. Instead, we have the strapline 'Life's too short to say no'. But 'Life's too short to say no' is a completely different message. Whereas the song acknowledges that there is something in the human spirit unsatisfied by the life of the world, the advert switches that around to suggest that it's urgent to grab as much stuff as possible as quickly as you can. Heaven is a place on earth, and it's run by First Choice Holidays. Just don't expect it to look quite like it does on screen, or for your destination to be reached swimming with turtles while all your clothes fall off.

---

24 'Life's too Short to say No', First Choice Holidays, extended version. See www.youtube.com/watch?v=JlsKRekgxTQ (accessed 08.01. 2020).

25 In an interview in *Rolling Stone*, 14 May 1970. See en.wikipedia. org/wiki/The_Seeker_(The_Who_song) (accessed 10.04.2020).

Of course, when it comes to using once-countercultural sounds to sell commercial products to the nostalgic, monied middle-aged middle class, the makers of the First Choice Holidays ad are only unusual in how late they are to the party. These 'creatives' aren't expecting their target demographic (who are much too young) to recognize the song or tap into a former, more idealistic self, just to reference something vaguely aspirational. This is very different from a generation ago, when Wrangler Jeans used a (subtle, skilful) storyline accompanied by a version of Jimi Hendrix's 'Crosstown Traffic' to suggest that the male wearers of their jeans were free lovers, 'more than just a number', or when Nurofen's employment of a version of Pink Floyd's 'Great Gig in the Sky', that influential lament about mortality, pointed instead towards a headache cure.[26] But the underlying message is just the same. Each advert takes the long vista of wonder, replaces it with a short-term luxury item – and tells you that's everything you've ever wanted.

Choose life?

In 1996 the film *Trainspotting*, directed by Danny Boyle and based on a book of the same title by Irvine Welsh, was released to general acclaim. It shows a British culture of post-Thatcher political, economic and personal disappointment. In its opening sequence it makes satirical play on the Deuteronomic strapline 'Choose Life', which formed a major part of the anti-heroin campaigns of the 1980s.[27] 'Choose Life' is glossed in relentlessly consumerist terms which hover round the demands of home and family: around job, children, TV, washing machine, mortgage; around 'DIY and wondering who the fuck you are

---

26 See www.youtube.com/watch?v=9RgKmkpm2EI for the 1990 Wrangler advert, which uses a reworked version of the 1967 Hendrix song. For the 1990 Nurofen advert, see www.youtube.com/watch?v= nvhkW20s5z4 (accessed 10.04.2020). 'The Great Gig in the Sky' appears on Pink Floyd, *Dark Side of the Moon* (1973).

27 Deuteronomy 30.19.

on a Sunday morning'. As the visual sequences switch from a frantic chase through drab streets, and a game of 5-a-side football watched by some bored young women and a baby, to the sight of Ewan McGregor passing out in a bleak interior while the soundtrack sings about a stripper, the voice-over comes to the point: that he's not about to choose life. And that he doesn't need to give any reasons for it. 'Who needs reasons when you've got heroin?'[28]

This is a kind of last gasp for anti-consumer romanticism. The film itself pushes back against its invertedly idealistic opening – the baby dies from neglect – but there's still a strong message about rejecting cheap fulfilment for the sake of something riskier, more intangible, more associated with the stopping of time. Just because it's grainy and drab doesn't mean it's not a piece of romantic refusal. (I can confirm from experience that so life-wreckingly naive a reading of the film was indeed possible.) The contempt for family responsibility also sounds very familiar: it's the working-class male rebellion expressed in hundreds of rock'n'roll lyrics from the previous generation.

The *Trainspotting* world still believes, in a soured sort of way, that individual fulfilment is the end of desire. But it is weirdly oblivious to the idea of heroin itself as the ultimate consumer good, a product that leaves nothing behind for your money except the need for more. Heroin is much more like the washing machine, CD player and so on than those famous opening credit lines can possibly acknowledge – but with no need for built-in manufacturer's obsolescence. Yet the logic of the *Trainspotting* credit sequence is that the romantic refusal of the addicted life is the only way to get out of the commercial curve, the only route towards a (lethal) truth.

Nothing else of the post-war romantic promise is left. Even the conviction that heroin use is anti-consumer is a lie. Romanticism and pop culture, harnessed after all to capitalist objectives in ever tighter loops. 'The road to pleasure is by the gates of death,' wrote St Benedict in the fifth century

---

28 See the clip here: www.youtube.com/watch?v=Fsk2IU9JQZo (accessed 08.01.2020).

(channelling the writer of Proverbs). And that's not as much fun as they tell you it's going to be.

'All your brain and body need'[29]

For the young of the long 1960s, freedom spoke through impulse and spontaneity, through an implicitly millenarian antinomianism, through a connected (if unfounded) belief in the essential innocence of the human spirit, and through the expression of sexual freedom as the ultimate sacred impulse. Transcendence found its voice not only through religious experimentation but through the exploration of mind-altering drugs. Aldous Huxley's *Doors of Perception* and de Quincey's *Confessions of an Opium Eater* were unwitting allies.

These values quickly met powerful capitalist structures and morphed into massive global businesses: drugs and pornography grew along with the music industry. The international trade in heroin, cocaine, cannabis and their derivatives reached into millions of ordinary lives. The rise of the internet gave pornography its current everyday dominance but the case was fought for it in the 1970s. Music-industry businessmen possessed and marketed the hopeful young for profit, then as now.

Our children negotiate a world dominated by these industries, taking in along with them the message that desires ought to be quickly satisfied rather than interrogated, harnessed or denied. At the same time a new, deeply alarmed culture of response makes on-the-back-foot attempts to regulate the consequences. The defensive work of regulation and the minimization of harm is itself now big business, and the impossible collisions between hedonism, free speech and social damage keep those underfunded institutions concerned with public welfare – schools, hospitals, police, social services, local government – very busy indeed.

---

29 Ian Dury, 'Sex and Drugs and Rock'n'Roll' (released from Stiff Records as a single in 1977).

Drug use and pornography have a lot in common, though they are only two of the many desires we buy and sell. One is illegal, the other legal. Pornography, the legal one, dominates the internet; both dominate the Dark Web. We have travelled a long way from the wilful innocence of John A. T. Robinson arguing, in 1970, that 'to deprive [a citizen] of the choice [to use pornography] is itself to deprave him [sic]'.[30] Now we have pornographic material insistently and addictively available today for every smartphone user, however young or vulnerable, so that increasing numbers of our children believe, as they emerge into adulthood, that sexual activity, and therefore their own growing bodies, are sites for display and consumer exchange. And the worst of it is that they are right.

Desire and gift

This is the history of desire in my lifetime. We have inherited some assumptions from 1960s 'liberation' about fulfilment, including the sexual kind. We see fulfilment as an exchange of gifts, but actually live it out within capitalist consumerism as a form of priced bargain. There's nothing recent, though, about the trade in bodies and how it battens on relationships. Marriage, along with slavery, traces that history too. So far as sex is concerned, Christianity attempted to solve the problem of sexual domination in two ways: by advocating virginity's freedoms (along with common ownership of a minimum of goods and an ascetic outlook upon other pleasures), so no one could be said to own anyone (or anything) else; and by reframing marriage as a form of mutually respectful gift. It didn't work out that way. The vowed religious life turned out to be a very big ask for human passions; the re-purposing of marriage as gift has had, to say the least, a patchy outworking.

---

30 John Robinson, 'Obscenity and Maturity', in *Christian Freedom in a Permissive Society* (London: SCM Press, 1970), quoted in Brewitt-Taylor, *Christian Radicalism*, p. 197.

But there are things Christians can say of the state we're in. That we should prize the gap between hope and fulfilment, desire and satisfaction, and cultivate living there within the disciplines of faith, hope and charity. That, as creatures, we do not possess. That we should not buy bodies. That it is worth taking time to interrogate why we think we want things – or people. That 'rights' are not the same thing as consumer goods.

Which are thoughts to take into the next chapter.

3

Looking

1 LOOKING AND TRUTH

The invitation to behold

Looking is more than seeing. It is a deliberate gaze. Employed in the imperative – 'Look!' – the word commands attention, invites understanding and hopes for responsive assent. It is serious. An invitation to look is an invitation to share a world of understanding. The translators of the Bible into English chose to translate the revelatory 'Look!' word with the archaic 'Behold!', derived from the Old English *behealden*, meaning ownership, in order to weight the command with proper gravity. To assent to the imperative 'Behold!' is to agree to hold, and thus to be held, by the change you are being invited to gaze upon. 'Behold the handmaid of the Lord,' says Mary to the angel, directing him to see in her an altered being with a transformed purpose.[1] A few months later, pregnant, she will tell her cousin Elizabeth, 'For behold, from henceforth all generations shall call me blessed.'[2]

Mary is not exactly asking Elizabeth to see something physical – even her baby is not yet visible to the outward eye. But she is calling Elizabeth as witness to a prophecy, to a transformed future with Mary as its chosen vessel of change. When worshippers – living their lives within the future generations

---

1 Luke 1.38. 'Behold' translates the Greek *idou* ('Look!'), which performs the same function but does not emphasize possession so strongly.

2 Luke 1.48b, and of course the 'Magnificat' said or sung every day at evening prayer in the Catholic and Anglican traditions.

she looks towards – repeat her words in their corporate evening prayer, they mark her prophecy's fulfilment.

It is momentous to step into the world of beholding. It confers a permanent change of perspective – and with it the obligations of change. The one who beholds is also beholden.

Refusing to look

Momentous, but not compulsory. Refusal is always possible; shared perspectives are not guaranteed. Modern politicians in interview often use 'Look!' – usually bolstered by filler words ('Yes; but look!') – to change direction, and frequently to deflect attention from the point of a question. It's the same conversational dominance move as the loudmouthed drunk ('yeah; but look; right?'). Those who employ 'Look!' to make sure of their audience (the politician, the drunk) attempt an unreliable shortcut to sharing an intimately agreed world view, but the fillers surrounding and softening the command reveal how slippery that relationship is. No one actually *has* to 'Look'.

Even the biblical 'behold' is as often used for truths ignored as for truths discovered. What separates out the Old Testament prophets from the people around them is not their personal virtue but the extent to which they cannot shut up about the truths they see. Refusing to speak truths may destroy them; speaking truths may break them anyway.[3] Not many of their hearers will want to help them bear such a weight.

In Matthew's Gospel Jesus ponders the gap between looking and assenting in a wry, melancholy response to a question. He has just told a story about a sower sowing seed, and when he has finished it and walked away the disciples ask why he preaches to the crowd through story, in the illustrative form we call the parable.[4] He replies with a quotation from the Scriptures: 'The reason I speak to them in parables is that

3 Exodus 3 and 4; 1 Kings 19; Isaiah 49.1–4; Jeremiah 1.1–10.
4 Matthew 13.1–23. See also Mark 4.1–20 and Luke 8.4–15.

"seeing they do not perceive, and hearing they do not listen, nor do they understand".[5]

His response walks a fine line between characterizing parables as a form of concealment and as a form of revelation. 'To you it has been given to know the secrets of the kingdom of heaven,' he says to them, 'but to [the crowd] . . . it has not been given'. 'For,' he adds, 'to those who have, more will be given and they will have an abundance, but from those who have nothing, even what they have will be taken away.'[6]

His remark sounds like harshness; but it simply describes the nature of refusal. It acknowledges the effects of using a form that requires responsive interpretative work from its hearers, hiding as it reveals and revealing as it hides. At the same time it assigns a remarkable, and gloomily realistic, weight to the predispositions of those who see and hear: that is, to what already exists in their hope or longing that might spark response. It hints that this honourable readiness to allow human beings their freedoms of refusal leaves them vulnerable to less scrupulous inner forces: greed, self-interest, pride, indifference (which is indeed the point of the sower story itself).

Jesus is marking his own distance from conversational dominance. Even though he begins his sower story with the commanding 'idou' ('Behold!'), the story form that follows draws back from command and into a world of responsive choices. What you bring to his narrative matters. Trust, curiosity, contempt, prejudice, or yearning – these emotions will shape your understanding. Will you spend time and care on the work of discovery, or will you lose interest and walk away?

Jesus expects that most people will walk away. What you've already got within you will dictate the shape of what you are prepared to receive. This is realistic rather than hopeful. Forget the centuries of academic argument about whether salvation is predestined by God's will; it is your own will and your own prejudice he is talking about, how high you are prepared to lift your own eyes, how long you are prepared to go on looking.

---

5 Matthew 13.13. Jesus is quoting Isaiah 6.9–10.
6 Matthew 13.11–12.

Unreceivable visions

This sorrowful exchange sits between a story in which seed that is sown becomes subject to the arbitrariness of terrain, weather, soil and predators, and an interpretation of that story that shows the 'seed' to be 'the Word of God', subject to the conditions into which it falls. Soil affects seed.[7] As he speaks with his disciples, Jesus reaches for the scriptural Word himself, and even says that the cool reception the crowd has given his sower story is actually its fulfilment. The Word he invokes and quotes is as it was received and heard by Isaiah, in the aftermath of an overwhelming vision of the presence of God, 'high and lofty, and the hem of his robe filled the Temple . . . the pivots on the thresholds shook at the voices of those who called, and the house filled with smoke'.[8]

> And [the voice of the Lord] . . . said, 'Go and say to this
>   people:
> "Keep listening, but do not comprehend;
> keep looking, but do not understand."
> Make the mind of this people dull,
>   and stop their ears,
>   and shut their eyes,
> so that they may not look with their eyes,
>   and listen with their ears,
> and comprehend with their minds,
>   and turn and be healed.'[9]

Still shaken by the sight he has seen, Isaiah finds it difficult to accept that it has become, in effect, impossible to share at the same time as he has received a command to share it. Is this how it will always be? 'How long, O Lord?' he asks. He is told that healing will not come until the whole land is desolate, ravaged and empty, felled like an oak: 'The holy seed is its

---

7 As I argued in Chapter 1 (pp. 11–12).
8 Isaiah 6.1–8.
9 Isaiah 6.9–11.

stump' (v. 13). Only desolation brings humanity to a living mode of seeing the divine glory, laments the divine voice.

Elsewhere in Scripture the question is turned around and asked by human beings of God's hiddenness.

> O Lord, how long shall I cry for help,
>   and you will not listen?
> Or cry to you 'Violence!'
>   and you will not save?
> Why do you make me see wrongdoing
>   and look at trouble?[10]

calls the prophet Habakkuk; and the psalmist also asks,

> How long will you forget me, O Lord; for ever?
> How long will you hide your face from me?[11]

The profound separation between humanity and God, which God's merciful readiness to allow free choice perpetuates, also separates seeing and hearing from recognizing and knowing. What is left in the gap is a cry of sorrow, echoing across from the divine to the human, the human to the divine.

Behold the man

And the desolation in the centre? What will bring together the lamenting voices of heaven and earth? There is one man, one place, one time. Jesus cries his reconciling cry in agony and abandonment as he dies upon the cross: '*Eli, Eli, lema sabachthani.*' 'My God, my God, why have you forsaken me?'[12] Characteristically, he inhabits Scripture, for this is the opening line of the twenty-second psalm. Barred from the goods of community, no longer personed, a still-breathing body under

---

10 Habakkuk 1.1–3a.
11 Psalm 13.1, *Common Worship*.
12 Matthew 27.46; Mark 15.34.

extermination outside the gates of the city, he cries out against his exile from the divine regard.

When the sparse Hebrew line was translated by St Jerome into the Latin of the Vulgate (and later by Miles Coverdale into the psalmody of the English Book of Common Prayer), a Christ-focused sense of the speaker prompted the insertion of a new phrase into the text: '*Deus, Deus meus,* respice me; *quare me dereliquisti*'; 'My God, my God, *look upon me*; why hast thou forsaken me?' In this version, the psalm still performs its liturgical work as Christ-icon in the tragic structure of Holy Week.

Jesus pleads with God to look upon him as a feeling subject, at a point when he has been formally made an object – an object of shame in the human drama of killing centring on him. The quiet editorial addition of 'look upon me' in Psalm 22.1 answers the moment in John's Gospel when the condemned Jesus is brought out in a royal robe and thorned crown and Pilate says to the crowd, 'Behold the man' (John 19.5). The robe and crown mock and pierce, and Pilate's own words drip with irony; but he reveals a truth that the crowd is too bloodily aroused to notice. The people see, but do not perceive; hear, but do not understand. God sees and hears, but is to his other self invisible.

The shame of crucifixion was supposed to exclude the criminal from human regard. Cicero offers the fastidious advice that 'the very name "cross" should not only be far from the body of a Roman citizen, but also far from his thoughts, his eyes and his ears'.[13] The inscription over Jesus' cross as it is described in John's Gospel literally runs, 'The King of the Jews – this!' It invites the occupiers' mocking comparison of Jewish kingship with the suffering thing spread broiling and panting before the watchers. These are the displays of an oppressive power, and Jesus' function in it is not merely as a personal but as a

---

13 Cicero, *Pro Rabirio Perduellionis* 5.16, discussed in Raymond E. Brown, *The Death of the Messiah*, vol. 2 (New York: Doubleday, 1994), p. 947.

political object of humiliation by the Romans for the whole Jewish people.

Blinded sight

At the crucifixion, heaven and earth look the same way – upon a suffering man – but see very differently. 'The Father turns his face away', asserts a modern devotional song, but this is poetic licence, a human view that God 'hides his face'. The Father may be silent, unseeable, but his looking is constant.[14] In the human gaze we mostly find tragic blindness; Pilate speaks an unknowing truth in 'Behold the man', and few see what they are invited to look at, in spite of every effort made by the dying Jesus to show them the redemptions of love and grief. As with the parable of the sower, what you bring shapes what you receive.

When Jesus speaks from the cross, his handful of words, across the different Gospels, not only claim his continuing personhood but express it in compassionate understanding. He sustains the dying man next to him.[15] He invites his grieving mother and his grieving friend to recognize in each other a relationship of healing.[16] He asks God to forgive all humanity its fatal tendency to loveless inattention.[17] Some of those watching his death ignore his claim to human connection, as with the man who, mishearing his cry of agony as a call for help from the prophet Elijah, says (effectively), let's not alleviate his suffering, let's wait instead and see whether there's any more entertainment to be got from his delusions.[18] But there are also individuals who recognize and witness to the dignity of his being, all the way to and beyond the end, from the women who stand far off because it is all they can do,[19] to the

---

14 Stuart Townend, 'How Deep the Father's Love for us'.

15 Luke 23.40–42.

16 John 19.25b–27.

17 Luke 23.34.

18 As it is told in Matthew 27.48–49. Compare the marginally more humane reaction in Mark 15.36.

19 John 19.25b; Luke 23.49; Mark 15.40–41; Matthew 27.55–56.

centurion who testifies to his divine identity as Jesus breathes his last breath.[20]

'Look, and be pierced'[21]

Zechariah's prophetic words transform our human looking, because they speak of seeing truly at last. 'When they look on the one whom they have pierced, they shall mourn for him, as one mourns for an only child, and weep bitterly over him, as one weeps over a firstborn . . . On that day a fountain shall be opened for the house of David.'

Even at this point of absolute desolation, the stump of the felled tree still contains the seed of life, and each speaker still looks towards that life's spring. It is not simply that the crucifixion stories are framed by the promises of resurrection. This moment of desolation has to be absolute, the promises void; the man we behold must die alone. Yet Jesus, dying and dead, testifies to enduring love as strongly and as really as the risen Jesus, whom Mary Magdalene will recognize through tears. God is there, suffering and looking upon suffering, inspiring the spring of healing sorrow, the pierced heart of a formerly murderous humanity. God is not absent but manifest and looking upon us from the most unexpected place.

---

20 Matthew 27.54; Mark 15.39; Luke 23.47.
21 Zechariah 12.10; John 19.37.

2 LOOKING AND REALITY

Keeping the lights on

Now that most people do not believe in God, no one is keeping them in perpetual sight. Yet people go on thinking and feeling increasingly anxiously about what keeps the soul's lights on, and especially what part looking and, crucially, being *looked at*, plays in that process. We have a need now constantly *to be seen*, so that we will spend much of each day recording for the eyes of others that the day happened. Is another's gaze the only sure guarantee of existence? If no one is looking, *are you really there*?

The twentieth century saw a thriving literature on 'Gaze' develop. Seeing and being seen became central to discussions on being, identity, desire and the interplay of social power. Work on the human gaze has played with the idea of a divine gaze, often by imagining God's absence (as in Jean-Paul Sartre's book *Being and Nothingness*[1]); but at the same time has become more locally interested in gaze as a site of desire and an expression of power. The inequalities of 'gaze' have been thought about in relation to masculine looking, imperial looking, the unequal gaze of doctor upon patient, or of a state upon its erring subjects.[2] The rise of interest in 'gaze' theory, its erotics and oppressions, follows the rise of photographic technologies: from the still camera image to film, TV, and now the democratized proliferation of online video.

Looking as act and thought

In these social conditions *scopophilia* – the desire to look without being seen – becomes a normal part of life. This unequal

---

1 Jean-Paul Sartre, *Being and Nothingness: An Essay on Phenomenological Ontology* (New York: Methuen, 1957 [1943]).

2 Laura Mulvey, 'Visual Pleasure and Narrative Cinema', *Screen* 16:3 (Autumn 1975); Edward Said, *Orientalism* (New York: Pantheon Books, 1978); Michel Foucault, *The Birth of the Clinic* (London: Tavistock, 1973 [1963]), and *Discipline and Punish* (New York: Pantheon Books, 1977 [1975]).

activity, basic to cinema, TV and the digital world, requires those who look to break the usual terms of a relationship encounter, reclassifying the person seen as an object, part of the interplay of the seer's own mind and emotions. Although we rarely define people *only* as objects – for it to be worth looking at an image you have to imagine a relationship with it – once you reclassify a sight as an object you blur the distinction between looking as an act in the world and looking as imaginative thought.

Vast amounts of modern looking take place on this complex boundary between looking as act and looking as thought. Our social responses to looking are therefore put under a good deal of strain. In some contexts we are completely reliant on saying that looking is not really an act in the world at all, so that when we look on simulated acts of violence or supposedly private sexual encounters within cinema we are not really *doing* anything at all, in the way that we would be if we sought out war zones for pleasure or spied on our neighbours in bed through a hole in the wall. As soon as it seems likely that we are watching real suffering, or real sex, the moral stakes go up.

Looking relies on a zone of *simulation* for its supposed harmlessness – a genre frame. If we know its genre we have a guarantee that what we see is representation, not reality: we know TV murder is acting, because we are watching a cop series. Yet the boundary between real and not-real is not stable. We live our imaginative lives and conduct our relationships among an enormous, proliferating wealth of domestically produced digital images, images used as currency for sharing real experience. We expect (especially in the UK[3]) to be routinely filmed on closed-circuit TV in all public places; closed-circuit footage is equally routinely shared publicly on digital platforms following public incidents such as stabbings. Our entertainment

---

3 Extrapolation from figures collected by Cheshire Constabulary in 2011 estimates that there are about 1.85 million cameras in the UK, in varying densities; and that a person in the average day will be filmed by approximately 70 cameras. See https://en.wikipedia.org/wiki/Closed-circuit_television#United_Kingdom (accessed 09.01.2020).

genres, both in professional filming and in the world of private image-sharing, mix real and not-real in order to blur the experiential boundary and heighten 'audience' reaction; reality shows and the mass of DIY contexts for staged naturalness mushroom because people react more intensely to sights they are encouraged to perceive as 'real'.

A mixed genre such as reality TV, or even your average selfie, is not direct experience; both rely on the simulations of genre. But, because they *are* mixed, they also rely on telling you that there is actually no simulation there at all. When the contestants on the dating reality show *Love Island* break down, or commit suicide (as several have), questions are asked about the psychological support they receive.[4] But the genre, by inviting everyone involved to treat what they see as really real, with real consequences in the real world, also invites its darker outcomes to be experienced as real trauma. If you turn your life into a game watched by millions, the outcome of the game (and your eventual expulsion from that intense, publicly watched game-space) has its powerful impact on your life. No wonder teenagers so eagerly consume dystopian narratives of young lives as gladiatorial contests such as *The Hunger Games*,[5] or as cut-throat sexual markets such as *The Jewel*.[6] They show something true about their own culture.

Our culture seems highly conflicted about whether looking is powerfully effective – some kind of real-world act – or completely ephemeral. We take the continual but highly mediated human

---

4 *Love Island*, in its 2018 series, is the most watched ever on ITV2, at 4,050,000 viewers. See https://en.wikipedia.org/wiki/Love_Island_ (2015_TV_series) (accessed 09.01.2020).

5 Suzanne Collins' *Hunger Games* trilogy, and its accompanying films, ranked second only to the Harry Potter series for its sales in August 2012, with 26 million copies sold worldwide. See en.wikipedia. org/wiki/The_Hunger_Games (accessed 09.01.2020).

6 The trilogy of *The Jewel*, by Amy Ewing, first published in 2014 by HarperTeens, is also, though more modestly, a 'bestseller', with translations into at least ten languages worldwide. The first book of the trilogy has 30,000 ratings on GoodReads. See www.goodreads.com/book/ show/40882262-the-jewel (accessed 09.01.2020).

gaze as inevitable, yet we appear to be gripped at the same time with a mixture of fear and desire at the thought of its absence.

The boundary: real and not-real

Of course modern life did not invent all this stuff. The representative arts (fiction, theatre, cinema, visual art), along with the real-world performances of liturgy and social ritual, have played with the boundary between real and not-real for millennia. But they've usually made those boundaries clear, the terms of engagement explicit.

Formal artefacts either claim the freedoms being imaginary or claim to record the absent real. The portrait painter recreates something that has vanished in real life: not just what someone looked like at a given moment, but something of what they have been through time. A photographer may balance 'moment' against 'history' in a different way, but the formal framing is still vital. The Gospels, of course, are formally mediated encounters with Jesus through a genre frame. Religious rituals of all kinds balance real against not-real by inviting people to participate on a porous but perfectly visible boundary between direct experience and representation. Theatre does something similar, though its reality-claims are different. All the same, it must always seem a little bit possible for theatrical emotion to spill into real life. Real-time collective performance, such as the pageant, the art installation,[7] the flash mob or the public execution, may blur the fictive/real boundaries even further. When we view a performance, we are protected from the trauma of completely raw looking; we need those boundaried protections to survive what we see. Yet directors, playwrights

---

7 For example, the installation *We're here because we're here* by Jeremy Deller and Rufus Norris (2016), where living figures (who were also members of the public, not professional actors) dressed as soldiers from World War One appeared unheralded at railway stations to commemorate the Battle of the Somme: www.telegraph.co.uk/art/artists/why-have-first-world-war-soldiers-been-appearing-around-the-coun/ (accessed 09.01.2020).

and artists toy with the danger of the boundary all the time, unsettling what audiences will experience, and how.

Looking as 'reall experiment'

The phrase 'reall experiment' comes from the seventeenth century.[8] A preacher talked about the 'reall experiment of mortality' in relation to funerals, using the phrase dramatically to connect up the process of dying with the coffined corpse an audience would look at. He was using 'experiment' with an older meaning than ours, to mean something more like 'experience', but a modern reader, coming across that phrase 'reall experiment', can't help hearing it with the overlay of its newer meaning.

For us, 'experiments' are primarily simulations of real conditions, set up artificially in order to make discoveries about the real as it occurs in the uncontrolled environment of the world. A 'real experiment', then, is almost a paradox: real and not-real at the same time. Experiment in the modern sense relies on there being a tightly defined boundary between mediated and unmediated experience, but (like reality TV) it also has to behave as if the boundary is either not there or not significant. For, if the experiment informs you primarily about the workings of the real, then the experiment defines your understanding of what the real is.

This shows us something our seventeenth-century forebears already knew: that the 'reall experiment of mortality' is a description of living as much as of dying. What might it mean to have to repeat something over and over in order to know the real when it arrives? To keep on and on starting again? What might that be, to have your little life rounded with a sleep – day after day? We do not have to be looking at the coffin of a relative or friend for the 'reall experiment' of mortality to be more than a reminder of what will be. It is the present cycle

---

8 Daniel Featley, *Threnoikos: The House of Mourning* (London, 1660), sig. A3v.

of one's own, finite breath, slipping away from now to then, continually noticed as if from a great distance.

'Screen time' and the past

As a child I was taken to the theatre as a great event, a day or evening out; and I read books almost all the time. But TV was the representational form that seemed to get closest to direct experience. In a strange way, TV *was* social life; it was how you knew yourself connected up. TV as it was then made the absent present because, with its few channels and its narrow viewing, everyone (just about) was watching the same thing at the same time. It showed things as if they were happening *right there and right now*: as if there were no awkward barrier between shared imagination and the really real. My friends at school were not reading themselves into other worlds but everyone watched *Marine Boy*, a world that for a short while I inhabited so continually and obsessively I sometimes believed the garden at home was really under the sea.[9] TV promised 'reall experiment'.

I was very interested in other ways of fixing experience. (My parents had a camera, and my uncle Trevor even had a cine-camera, or 'telly on the wall', but these were sparse, magical events, adult-controlled.) Having found reading, I would try out authorial forms in my head as a way of making sure I continued to exist. *She fastened the stiff brown straps of her sandals. Her socks were grey and would not stay up.* Children's books then used the past tense and the third person, so my narration *was* a God's-eye view, retrospective, authoritative. This suited me fine. I wanted to be something more reliable than a subject moving tracelessly through time. Practising on the patterns of dressing, tidying, washing, or walking from place to place, I learnt that unselective narrative was too detailed.

---

9 See https://en.wikipedia.org/wiki/Marine_Boy; www.thechestnut.com/marine.htm (accessed 09.01.2020). It was broadcast on BBC1 in 1969.

It died on me as it lost shape. I worried a lot about what was happening to the experiences as they went by; how would I manage to remember them all, who would remember if I forgot, if narrative didn't work how would I keep my life, *where did it all go?*

I made memory experiments, concentrating hard on the sight of *this moment* – and then *this moment.* I still retain a few willed images of this kind: looking back at myself from the long mirror, wearing a school summer dress my mother was sewing for me, in green and white check, with the tacked, unhemmed skirt still romantically long; tumbling about in the boot of a car with my brother, two other boys, some muddy wellies and an old rug as we bumped along a bleak and shabby narrow road; the page of a 'Ladybird' picture book containing a clear pastel image of a baby's brush and comb; the brown and yellow criss-cross of bars and ropes against the sides of the infant school hall associated with the limp, suspicious taste of a caterpillar-nibbled lettuce.

But television. Television did look like the answer to my question. I thought it could not lie. It seemed to promise a recall that would be transparent, as frictionless as experience but reliably *recorded* as experience refused to be. My imagination began to provide images it called memory and yet were seen from a camera's-eye view. In the second memory I've recorded, the one about being in the boot of a car, I remember it partly from the outside: I am visible alongside the three boys. It was a third-person narration with an imaginary cameraman. And I can remember floating down the stairs, feet above the treads by several inches, steering myself lightly with fingers against the wall, angled upwards as if I was watching myself descend. I was *televising.*

My fantasies of a filmed self-narrative spooling backwards through time were just that – fantasies, like the equally vivid false memory of myself, a boy, and powerful, swimming purposefully with my dolphin companion through the undersea heather of the garden. The external eye was an internal device for performing self-consciousness, not a mode of being. My idea of television had little to do with the real televisual craft of domestic, strictly genred framing, as mannered as opera, as clunky as pantomime, as resolutely demotic as a dictator's speechifying. Television to me was a comforting metaphor for a fully recorded, fully *seen* mental existence which provided a way of understanding my separate selfhood in time and space. The thoughts I had about who I might be used the techniques of visual and told narrative; they took their place with equally urgent inquiries about where I had been before I was born (a shining, white-draped yet modernist-boxy storeroom, somewhere that might have been found in the clinical heaven of *A Matter of Life and Death*, a film I had not yet seen), and how I was going to stand to wait out the time before I discovered what would happen after I died. I kept all these thoughts in a place in my head to which I deliberately limited my visits; they gave me a kind of mad feeling but were very tempting. They felt dangerous.

Of course it was all impossible. I knew perfectly well that no one was filming the days of my life, that the narratives of my head fixed nothing, impressed no one. (God, in whom I believed, wouldn't be interested; unpredictably powerful yet deeply preoccupied, he had a lot of other stuff to do.) My fantasies were basically a way of managing to be alone. Human life was neither a library nor a massive multi-dimensional film. Everyone's experience just slipped backwards and away – perhaps into a land of nowhere, the white box room of never-having-been. The inner story was just a handy means for connecting up with love in moments of separation or fear. It wasn't a real thing – then. Like imagining family and friends weeping over your coffin, it was a way to have weight and value in a big, fast-moving, indifferent world.

Mirrors of desire

That was then. Then, the internal visual narrative, poised ambiguously between real and not real, along with its imagined, endlessly sympathetic and attentive audience, stayed in a place of unambiguous privacy: inside your head.

But now? Now the relationship between inside and outside is utterly changed, because what was once only imagined is now declared to be proved.[10] The promise of the digital world that we now inhabit is that the inward spool can be *realized*, made available to a pool of watchers as large or small, as selective or unselective, as you opt to make it. The process is designed to imitate the impulsive swiftness of thought, clicking and thinking beguilingly aligned, the window to your soul opened wide and deliberately to the outside breeze of a world's gaze.

It seems as if the metaphor of video as life's 'reall experiment' is today more real than it is experiment, an analogue to life itself so close that the one melts into the other, experiment to experience. The temporal screen is a mirror of desire nestling in your back pocket whose flat, resistant surface offers to dissolve on command into something else. It will become a yielding pool into whose memories you may dive until they rise up real around you, and you wander invisible within a world that both is, and is not, your own.

When, in the 1990s, J. K. Rowling imagined those two magical artefacts, the Mirror of Erised and the Pensieve, they had no real-world analogues, and the adverts on London's escalators could not wave back.[11] Now they can, and the Mirror of Erised is not a hidden temptation in a dusty room but an everyday domestic device possessed by almost 5 billion people worldwide.[12] The narrative point of the Mirror, in Rowling's books, is that it reflects the watcher's 'deepest, most desperate' desires; this is what makes it dangerous. Usually it shows either the impossible or something you are very unlikely ever to possess. It is never explained who made it, or why – that would interfere with its moral function in a story that is about the building of character in adversity.

---

10 'What is now proved was once only imagin'd': William Blake, *Auguries of Innocence* (1803).

11 The Mirror of Erised and the Pensieve are both emotionally significant magical devices in the world of the Harry Potter books by J. K. Rowling.

12 See www.statista.com/statistics/274774/forecast-of-mobile-phone-users-worldwide/ (accessed 09.01.2020).

In this it is in fact different from the modern mobile phone, a device with makers and a history, folded into an industry with one overriding intention: to keep you watching anything at all that might sell you something. While the Mirror of Erised is a narrative device that only exists to test your soul, the digital world the mobile brings to your hand is not indifferent to your subjectivity and probes your desires in every way possible, but your desires are not exactly the point – nor are they exactly yours. A truly impossible desire is not commercially interesting, and an unlikely desire hardly more so (though unlikely desires do offer opportunities for marketing illusions). This is mostly about small-scale matches between urge and achievable delivery. Desire is only a means towards multiple transactions; your soul is no more than a site to be mined for profit. There only needs to be an approximate correlation between what you want and what you are offered – just enough to beckon you towards other transactions – until what you want is actually being dictated by the profit motive and not by the shape your desires might have taken without the nudge.[13] All that is solid melts into data.[14]

Disembodied seeing

The online world is not a world of touch, but of sight. Human beings in the real world use sight as orientation, to fix the body's physical context and perspective. It is *empirical*. When we see in the real world, with our clever eyes that adjust focus and range more subtly than the most sophisticated of cameras, it reminds us of the limitations of the body: of height, touch, distance, terrain, strength.

---

13 Shoshana Zuboff, *The Age of Surveillance Capitalism: The Fight for a Human Future at the New Frontier of Power* (London: Profile Books, 2019); James Williams, *Stand Out of our Light* (Cambridge: Cambridge University Press, 2018).

14 Karl Marx originally said, 'All that is solid melts into air.'

The world of represented sights is very different, frequently magically so. You can float among the stars, enormous in your visual range; walk under the sea in pressures impossible for the human lungs and heart; gaze into the heart of a volcano; disappear inside the body of a whale or even a flea. Once upon a time such imagining belonged in the microcosm of the imagination, the world of inward seeing that John Donne said made human beings 'a diminutive to nothing'.[15] In that world the physical body is ghostly, strangely unsituated; our perspective is impossible. The image-world in which we are immersed has no room for our bodily presence, and the mind doesn't know, therefore, whether to categorize that image-world as realer, or less real, than the limited flesh it cannot accommodate.

That is quite significant even with 'straight' film, the kind of thing you might see on *Blue Planet*, film that has been creatively edited but has ethical limits well short of faking stuff. *Blue Planet* goes out of its way to remind its watchers how difficult it was to capture its images by filming the process of filming, a guarantee of solid-gold truth. Once you add the remarkable possibilities of convincing visual fictions via computer-generated imagery to the mix of watched stuff, the mind's orientations become confused. The growing modes of virtual reality will disrupt its perspective even further. The drive towards the attention-grabbing hyperpalatable faked image adjusts the mind towards the fast, the bright, the astonishing, the continuously sublime or terrifying or saccharine. The slower modes of real experience become difficult to wait for: tasteless, boring, drab and slow.

And the mind conditioned into such a state begins to ail. It stops being able to imagine things on its own. It can't settle down to the slow work of noticing or negotiate the friction-filled world of *things*. As people attempt to adjust, YouTube fills up with stuff happening slowly: rain falling in a single spot, someone ironing and folding clothes, relaxation videos, the growing genre of ASMR (autonomous sensory meridian response)

---

15 John Donne, *Devotions upon Emergent Occasions, and severall steps in my Sicknes* (1624), meditation 4.

videos. The cure for watching something becomes watching something else.

The digital gaze

Much is being written about the predations of the 'attention economy' upon human sensibility.[16] This is not the place to rehearse the reasons *why* the digital world behaves as it does, troubling and compelling though they are, but to look at some unanticipated effects of the screen realm of 'reall experiment' into which we gaze and fall. Our eyes take us through the mobile mirror into a place that both is and is not the world, a place in which we are both real and imaginary, both invisible and ferociously visible, apparently traceless yet infinitely trackable, where forgotten ephemera take up permanent existence and can appear at any time with the damning solidity of something engraved on tablets of stone.

Audiences for our digital thoughts are not those stable, archetypal entities of loving mother/distant father my five-year-old self imagined, empathetic, understanding, wise. They are, however, powerful. They may be agents of the law or the state looking for signs of subversion or transgressive guilt. They may be market researchers reading patterns of behaviour for commercial gain. If they are private persons, they will have urges of their own to discharge, their own 'deepest, most desperate desires' to express; not only sympathy and conversational connection (though those are important blessings of digital communication) but hatred, resentment, fury, impulses to murder or to rape, envy, lust, despair and contempt. In the shadow-world of the digital realm, these emotions, which cannot help but exist in private feeling, find their outlet into a kind of thought-scape whose not-realness appears to give anyone permission to vent them on the array of apparent ghosts in the internal machine.

---

16 Matthew Crawford, *The World Beyond Your Head: On Becoming an Individual in an Age of Distraction* (London: Penguin, 2016).

And then someone in the actual, real world – a child, perhaps, finding growing up hard, or a young man wondering what good his existence does, what weight it has – will take that step towards suicide, or despair, or mental breakdown; or perhaps a real politician will really be stabbed at her regular constituents' surgery – but you never knew them, so how could any of that be your fault? And the business model that has noticed that outrage generates more traffic than conversational harmony, and that therefore outrage should be encouraged – it's not their fault, either? The social media forum – well, it's just a platform for whatever human beings want to put onto it, isn't that right? That's freedom; and we like freedom. The whole digital world is built on freedom.

The ideology of the digital realm is an (implicitly masculine) one of liberation, progress and personal power, one that assumes the self to be sovereign, with a universe of information there for the taking. And that is true: the cosmic scale of information *is* there, in all its variousness and beauty and richness, bringing to a great mass of people sights and knowledge once the province of the few. The dream of the digital world is of an almost infinitely extensible environment through which users may wander as invisibly and untraceably as they want to be, without the trammels of accountability that attend real-world journeys and encounters. Within this sort of rhetoric the wandering self and its desires is endogenous, a self-sufficient system, making choices according to a logic over which it has complete control, including the beguiling choices of self-disclosure or self-disguise. Such an idea construes the internet as a form of internal space, a world of the mind, in which every thought is both realized and yet as inviolably traceless as unvoiced thoughts have always been.

At the same time people recognize the digital world as sharing real-world features that contradict some of these assumptions. They assume that identities asserted, opinions expressed and histories shared will be recognized, heard and seen. They know, too, that the things they post actually have a true longevity that reveals the events of the outer world to be the real ephemera. The things you say and do in outer experience disappear; but when they appear in the digital world, they last and last. The dead still speak on Facebook, often to invite friends to their funerals.

This looks like the fixing of the self that living in time does not allow, the recall of experience from the abyss of the continually vanishing past. The digital world holds out a form of *anamnesis*, not-forgetting. For good or ill, it offers, to your every posted thought or action, immortality. But don't expect forgiveness to be part of the package. This world of eternity is a world of human judgement; no mercy is guaranteed.

Nor is it really the case that the *experience* of the digital world is either endogenous or as fast as a thought. It is true that connection has the capacity to be extremely fast, and that we may click as we think; but the environment of adverts, pop-ups and hostile comment that we navigate makes our progress anything but untrammelled, and our choices anything but free. It is more like the way I remember walking along the average street used to be in my teens. In the digital version of that lost 1970s street, as you travel towards the destination you intended for yourself your mind-body is constantly nudged, goosed, felt up, pinched, flicked, stroked, slapped, grabbed, catcalled, kerb-crawled, obstructed, hooted at, faced down. Such public intrusions would never now be tolerated in the real world (not here, at any rate, though women and girls the world over suffer them, and worse, every day); but the digital one has no civilities to protect you from everyday assault. You walk that virtual road through an incessant mass of greedy watchers, hoping to be ignored. You live in the Gaze. The internet does not feel like privacy to me. It feels like exposure.

3 LOOKING AND THE SOUL

'The One with the Free Porn'

The first showing of the *Friends* episode 'The One with the Free Porn' was on 26 March 1998.[1] Characteristically, it made its jokes with shifts of register, disrupting viewers' genre expectations by getting them to compare the romantic and the pornographic across the plot lines. The background to the main storyline had New York room-mates Joey and Chandler glued to a porn cable channel which they had accidentally accessed for free and didn't dare switch off in case they lost it, while in the foreground their friend Ross was caught up in an across-continents romcom with his English girlfriend Emily. The final gag, though, landed with Joey and Chandler, who were already taking shamefaced refuge in the next-door flat from the relentless porn playing all day in their own. In the episode's last two minutes, they finally cracked and switched the porn off. Seconds later, the show's end shot saw them switching it on again.

That, too, was then. Screen pornography was mainly a cable and videotape/DVD business, with upfront payment, which was why Joey and Chandler felt they couldn't switch the channel off when they happened on it for free. There was plenty of porn around in and before the 1990s, but the user had to put some mild effort into finding it; payment in advance and its possible interactions also provided a kind of decision-boundary. The shape that twentieth-century screen porn took on imitated mainstream genres; the porn we dimly see playing throughout the *Friends* episode is indeed confusable with screen romance. This is not just because of the censorship constraints of sitcom viewing, but because familiar narrative frames really did provide something porn needed. Yes, settings with a bit of built-in variation and delay for an otherwise reductive mode, but also a necessary piece of viewer-orientation that cloaked, or at any rate contained, the content with a reassuring sense of the

---

1 See https://en.wikipedia.org/wiki/Friends (accessed 09.01.2020).

normative. It is this that disorients Joey and Chandler when they have had the channel running for days on end, because their real-life settings of everyday normality – the women serving them in the pizza parlour or the bank – have begun to look only like an opening for a porn narrative. They find this stressful, even upsetting; but the episode's final, slightly sour joke is on them, because they can't switch it off.

Things have changed. Today pornography provision is more or less entirely digital, and 'mainstream' porn is largely free-to-use, designed to be almost as quick and easy as thought in its access. The films are short; the sites that offer access to them are set up to 'bombard the viewer with multiple images really fast – like "click on this!" "click on this!", with moving images, and bells and whistles, kind of Vegas-strip-style'.[2] The pay-to-use adult packages of the past (bought direct from specialist production companies, with traceable business transactions) still exist here and there, for example for the hotel market; but they are not the norm. Like newspapers, they are in trouble. The new digital model built itself up on 'amateur' or pirated internet content with little that was traceable or accountable. Users will not know whether the people they see have been paid, or how much, or what level of coercion actors have experienced, or how old they are. More recently the digital hubs that distribute porn have become more willing to pay for content, but there is still a real cloudiness about sources and conditions for making porn.[3] Porn is expensive to make unless you exploit your actors, and in a free-to-use market it's challenging for content providers to recoup their outlay.[4]

2 Shira Tarrant, author of *The Pornography Industry: What Everyone Needs to Know* (Oxford: Oxford University Press, 2016), interviewed in *Atlantic Monthly* on 4 April 2016. See www.theatlantic.com/business/archive/2016/04/pornography-industry-economics-tarrant/476580/ (accessed 09.01.2020).

3 Tarrant, *Atlantic Monthly*.

4 See www.theatlantic.com/notes/2016/04/what-it-costs-to-film-a-porn-video/477048/ (accessed 09.01.2020).

There is an awful lot of digital porn. In 2018 one of the world's biggest free-to-use digital sites, Pornhub, had 33.5 billion visits worldwide, an increase of 5 billion on the previous year, with daily visits up at almost 100 million and a volume of content provided to match demand. As its breezy analytics reporter remarks in the 2018 'Year in Review', that means that 'if you were to start watching 2018's videos after the Wright brother's [sic] first flight in 1903, you would still be watching them 115 years later'.[5] Most of it (80 per cent) was watched on a tablet or smartphone; the desktop share of the markets is shrinking each year. The UK was second after the USA in the top 20 countries using Pornhub's services.

Genre is still a very significant aspect for porn, and romance an important, recently expanding label, especially among the female users of porn who now make up a significant minority of the market (29 per cent and growing). Pornhub looks at genre through the lens of search terms, as well as its own unvarying (and therefore defining) global categories. The marketing interest is of course in the shape and fluctuations of users' desires, and the search terms data show a mix of genre frames that follow mainstream media-rooted interests closely: reality shows, celebrity culture, the music scene, sport, politics, films and cartoons, video games, anime, cosplay and dating apps. In the UK in 2018 the search term 'Elastigirl' from the children's movie *The Incredibles* challenged even the characteristically British staples of 'Bondage', 'Big Tits' and 'Love Island'. 'Life imitates art, and eventually porn imitates everything,' remarks Pornhub's analyst, adapting a remark of Oscar Wilde's.[6] And if 'everything' means all the relentlessly stylized outputs of multiple-screen media, the analyst is right.

Looking through the search terms lens, or indeed Pornhub's own '100 Categories', gives a curious, skewed perspective on

---

5 All data is taken from 'Pornhub 2018 Year in Review', posted 11 December 2018.

6 Oscar Wilde, *The Decay of Lying* (1889). Wilde wrote that 'Life imitates Art more often than Art Imitates Life'. In context, it's a risky allusion.

the inner life of users of so-called 'mainstream porn'. But this strange hall of mirrors is really only the blandest of shop windows. The business model for Pornhub, as a free-to-use digital site with a massive customer base, relies on there being something to advertise beyond free porn for which their customers might pay upfront. Pornhub is owned by the firm MindGeek, which owns several other porn businesses, and indeed operates something close to a monopoly on digital porn.[7] Because porn cannot advertise on non-pornographic mainstream platforms, advertising must all happen once users have come to the site via a search term – though there is also an established and successful practice of posting non-disclosive teasers on ordinary sites as inducements to visit. Once there, users will encounter advertising for other sites probably owned by the same company, and the algorithms that track preferences will be working out what kind of paid-for service this particular user might be nudged towards.

Thus pay-to-view extreme and specialist viewing is a significant indirect aspect of the digital porn business model. It begins to answer the question of what content providers get out of it: rich data about the direction of customer preferences, within a huge customer base. These preferences can be met, and indeed shaped, through pay-to-use content that offers a more intense, more extreme version of that preference. A number of 'mainstream' categories ('Teen', the 'College Girls' category popular in India, or Japan's 'Japan School') appear to be beckoning in a troubling direction. Others promise stylized violence, ('Gangbang'); and the range and ranking of blandly offered ethnicity categories are also a bit thought-provoking, particularly once you know that actors of some ethnicities are much more likely to be trafficked or exploited than the average white porn star.

---

7 Tarrant quotes a 2014 estimate that MindGeek owns eight out of the ten biggest porn sites, a figure that MindGeek says is too high. Tarrant also points out that monopolies in big tech-based businesses, of which porn is one, are not really being challenged, and that the porn industry's business model should be more transparent.

There are some identifiable ethnic slumming trends: the UK with 'British chav',[8] the French with 'Arab', the Germans with 'Turkish' (the Austrians, when not looking up people in uniforms, have a mystifying weakness for 'German Neighbour'); and the USA seems to have a fairly complicated relationship with its racial inheritance. Leaving aside the sexual politics of the world of porn (something that is clearly in flux in a number of ways, but with its straightforward misogyny and racism not yet noticeably undermined[9]), part of the 'everything' porn imitates is the cultural prejudice of the world from which it borrows its settings; objects of fear and attraction for its users are exposed with minimal comment in the company's data.

The Pornhub 'Year in Review' has no section that discusses its business model, ethical limits or advertising policy, though it gestures sketchily towards the welfare of its users in references to its 'Pornhub Sexual Wellness Center'. Like abstinent drug barons, porn companies are perkily clear that what you look at, and what that makes you think and feel, is your own responsibility. Yet the business model is one that aims to shape and even intensify what users think and feel (and how frequently they think and feel it) for commercial gain. Because of the use of algorithms based on customer data, Tarrant points out, 'you're being spoon-fed a limited range of pornography based on the keywords you use'. She adds:

> Online-porn users don't necessarily realize that their porn-use patterns are largely molded by a corporation. We talk about the construction of wants and needs in other aspects of the economy, but that applies just as well to pornography . . . it really shapes our views . . . about how we understand agency and desire.

---

8 'Chav' is a disrespectful slang term for the London diaspora of white English working class living in Essex and parts of Kent, caricatured as loud, ignorant, sexy, mouthy and given to cheap personal display.

9 The categories most watched by women on Pornhub divide sharply between 'romance' and strong participation in the stylized male-to-female violence and constraint enjoyed by male viewers. It seems that the 'male gaze' isn't weakening its hold on us just yet.

Before the domestication of the internet, porn addiction was not a widespread or commonly acknowledged phenomenon. Those unfortunates suffering it either directly or indirectly via a family member were more likely to encounter amusement, incomprehension or even a strange distaste – as if such distress were illiberal – than understanding. Porn itself, of course, was then not so insistently visible and not so easy to procure. Nowadays it is a high-profile issue. In my diocese, the Diocese of Ely, its annual 'Ministry Development Review' form for clergy has 'addiction to pornography' listed as a difficulty for which help might be sought, along with the other common life-wreckers: mental health problems, domestic problems, debt and alcoholism. In this, the diocese simply follows best practice. Pornography is a major issue for mental health because its business patterns encourage obsessive use, and people with any kind of vulnerability (not to mention the teenagers and children who will, and do, find their way to the massive volume of internet porn but are of course absent from its published analytics) quickly find themselves in a loop with no easy exit. The joke on Joey and Chandler was played on them in a world where porn was perceived as scarce and expensive. When it was freely available, their ability to live normally was quickly impaired. Nowadays everyone, potentially, has a free porn channel in their back pocket, playing all day, every day. The choice they are faced with is not about switching it on. It is about switching it off.

Do people switch porn off? Porn companies' analytics look, of course, at patterns of use: times of day, patterns of use within the week, and outside events that affect traffic. Although, as Pornhub's analyst remarks, 'people are pretty regular when it comes to their masturbation schedule', live communal events such as the 2018 royal wedding,[10] national elections, large sporting events (or even, in a Catholic country like Italy, the Feast of the Assumption) cause significant drops in traffic. Friday is the day of lowest use, because people

---

10 The search term 'Meghan Markle', however, did very well in 2018.

have things to do together in their lives. Patterns for watching porn reflect patterns of being alone with your smartphone. It is something for times of emptiness. Porn's most popular watching day, therefore, is Sunday. 'From sunrise to sunset this day is holy', sang the priest from the altar as I pondered this piece of data, her young voice soaring in controlled flight across the sparse congregation and up into the heights of Ely Cathedral, 'and though the night will overtake this day, you summon us to live in endless light'.

Or, of course, you could spend the morning watching 'British chav'.

The soul's windows

In the Gospels, Jesus has very little to say about sex. But he makes several remarks about desires. In the Gospel of Matthew he says that 'everyone who looks at a woman with lust has already committed adultery with her in his heart'.[11] And in the Gospel of John he saves the woman taken in adultery from stoning by saying to her potential killers, 'Let anyone among you who is without sin be the first to throw a stone at her.' One by one, 'starting with the elders', they put their stones down and walk away.[12]

When Jesus is talking about the disposition of the heart, he is thinking the same way. It's the 'evil intentions' which 'come out of the heart' that corrupt people, not the breaking of community rules.[13] Or there's the saying that uses looking as its main metaphor. 'The eye is the lamp of the body,' he tells those around him. 'So, if your eye is healthy, your whole body will be full of light; but if your eye is unhealthy, your whole body will be full of darkness. If then the light in you is darkness, how great is the darkness!'[14] The 'health' of the eye isn't, of course,

---

11 Matthew 5.28.
12 John 8.7.
13 Matthew 15.16.
14 Matthew 6.22–23.

about whether someone has 20/20 vision. It is about the way that what is in your heart colours – or shadows – how you see what you see. It is an utterly different way of understanding human perception from the modern idea of a detached entity whose eye is always reliable in its judgements – that mask of self-image behind which hides the irrational, anxious, erratic being observed by behavioural psychologists and exploited by marketing strategists.

In what Jesus says about the heart he gives most weight to desire itself: he sees inner feelings – lust or envy – as defining someone's relationship with the outside world. Jesus' remark about adulterous desire is characteristically impossibilist; he seems to be pointing out that all humans feel this – and also feel other vicious and destructive emotions for which there is no expressive room in a real life serving God and neighbour. Holiness begins, then, with refusing to become someone else's judge. Not as a mythical 'detached observer' but in *recognition*.

And that's the beginning of a long, a lifelong, task, impossible without the grace of God, of learning to see with a 'healthy eye', for which recognition is the first step. It is a school of the heart. 'How can you say to your neighbour, "Let me take the speck out of your eye", while the log is in your own eye?' asks Jesus extravagantly. 'You hypocrite! First take the log out of your own eye and then you will see clearly.' Clear sight, from which issues clear action, is not available to those who have angled themselves into a position where they have to *pretend* that they can see.[15]

When the woman taken in adultery is brought before Jesus, her sin seems to have divided her from her fellow men, the gulf set between guilty culprit and innocent accusers. She has become objectified, half-human: something upon which they can vent lethal fury, frustration and envy. It's possible to read this scene – where a group of men are united in wishing to hurl stones at a woman found in bed with another man until the injuries kill her – as one in which she has stopped being a separate human being in their eyes. She hovers between real

---

15 Matthew 7.4–5.

and not-real, a simulacrum of all that they hate and fear in themselves. Stoning was a punishment in law, but no one could stone someone dispassionately. Stoning serves a fearful righteousness that can only defend its borders by identifying a repository for the whole community's flaws – and then destroying it.[16]

Jesus helps the men notice what is making them so angry. He shows them that the destructive desire that they try to destroy by stoning the woman is their own desire. It is futile to hope that destroying her will destroy it. They will still be left dealing with themselves. They relied on separating her act of adultery from their thoughts about it, but the problem lies in what is already in their hearts. Perhaps the men even notice that their destructive desire was the fuel for their anger, that they were not seeing with a clear eye. They go away one by one to think about it, and leave the woman standing alone with Jesus, who asks, '"Have they condemned you? . . . neither do I".' And he suggests to her that she needs to live differently now – not because she made the elders want to kill her, but because she is hurting her own soul. 'Go, and do not sin again.'

Jon Ronson, in his book *So You've Been Publicly Shamed*, quotes a victim of a Twitter shaming as saying, 'I'd never had the opportunity to be an object of hate before. The hard part isn't the hate. It's the object.'[17] His book shows people – the shamers rather than the shamed – who look wonderingly at the destruction they were able to wreak and say, but I am just normal, I love my children and my partner, then . . . 'you turn around and suddenly you are at the head of a pitchfork mob'.[18] The mixture of real and not-real, of solidity and ephemerality in online communication, seems to be destabilizing people's sense of what they are doing. When online expression feels very like yelling a thought, or a feeling, into a space that still

16 See René Girard, *La Violence et le Sacré* [*Violence and the Sacred*] (Paris: Bernard Grasset, 1972).

17 Jon Ronson, *So You've Been Publicly Shamed* (London: Picador, 2015), p. 292.

18 Ronson, *Shamed*, p. 47.

acts a little like the inside of your own head and yet is full of people who answer back, it seems to bring forth raw versions of deep and extreme desires, intensified by fear and hung on to a pure persona of judgement, behind which the speaker can hide. The match between that persona and the person who might speak in the real world is never complete, but also never severed. A persona says and does what it says and does online, a ghost in the machine. But the person in the real world is attached to it by an unbreakable chain.

Hauntings

The online mirror of desire is distorted. The face that looks back at you from your online actions and preferences is a photofit, constructed in part out of bits of other people and made to assist your capture. It is a haunting, a creature of the uncanny valley, searching for your weaknesses. The rules that determined its making were crafted by strangers who do not care about your soul; they may wish not to be evil but they are not in the business of doing good. If outrage makes traffic, then outrage is a neutral, useful thing. It would be handy to have more of it. Likewise they have no moral issue with any desire or preference, but they do have uses for them. So that, in relation to porn for example, the terms you feed in will be vital to the culture and business model of the porn market exactly insofar as they can sharpen the hunger of that market. How data is generated from the external world, its prejudices and fears and longings, is a matter purely for sales analysis, because that analysis will point towards future shaping of customer preferences. And, as a customer, your preferences are customer preferences, nudged, predicted, developed. The shapes your desire takes are neither as spontaneous nor as autonomously chosen as they might seem to be.

It's easy to forget this when there is such a proliferation of stuff apparently set up to provide a match to every inchoate urge of the private mind. Reading a category list for porn viewing can seem like looking at a telepathic card index of unexpressed or inexpressible fantasy, the stuff civil society doesn't have room for or the shadow side of its expectations – a place to put anger and disappointment and longing and loss and fear, a place that might feel safely unreal, absolutely possessed on easy terms and yet never quite bringing its objects within reach. The whole point of porn for the one looking is . . . the one looking. No one else is there. Fantasies of connection, or action, or agency of any kind, are set up for a disappointed waking, which is both safety and let-down: *it was only a dream.* Though the actors of porn films have lives and needs and histories and childhoods and identities, that stuff is hidden; they are set up only to be the outward and visible sign of the customer's inward and spiritual thought. And that feels like a safe place on which to project extreme feeling. Perhaps it even is; most fantasy rapists don't turn into real ones.

So the creature of your internet preferences is not you. The online eye holding you in place is neither infinitely knowledgeable nor wonderfully kind. The truth it shows you is a clumsy simulacrum dressed in your identity. It may show you a person you are afraid of being; or may show you someone you know you cannot be.

Yet it is powerful. Its gaze changes who you are becoming. The logic of nudge marketing is rather like the logic that governs successful metaphor: its power comes as much from unlikeness as from likeness.[19] The person who finds himself looking at a variety of porn or a vista of violence to which he hadn't quite intended to assent is finding his excitement in the *difference* between its extremity and his understanding of his own desires, even though the algorithm will have detected and built upon patterns of similarity. But a sight once seen has its own trauma and exerts its own patterns of change upon the one who sees. Seen cannot ever revert back to unseen.

---

19 This quality of metaphor is considered carefully and at length in Adam B. Seligman and Robert P. Weller, *How Things Count as the Same: Memory, Mimesis and Metaphor* (Oxford: Oxford University Press, 2019), pp. 78–98.

Although a scopophilic society requires people to believe that they can create stable conditions under which whatever they see will leave them essentially unchanged, fully in control of the identity and preferences of the 'I' who decides to look, this is not true. And everyone knows that. Although people will not reliably become murderers by watching murder on screen, they will become people with their inner vision stocked with murders, and must therefore find a way to categorize those murders as untraumatic.

Managed successfully, this may even be disappointing. People watch stuff in order to feel things. Every kind of seeing, from the most artificial to the most faithful, plays with the boundary between fictive and real encounter in order to *make something happen*. Sights are billed as life-changing – even though at the same time we receive implicit assurance that their life-changingness is optional, temporary.

The expanding world of mixed real/not-real, whether in the mix of CGI with real footage, or in entertainment experiments with real lives, or image-heavy social media narratives of relentless success, or the posting of mobile or webcam video, or the shift in flash-mob culture between light-hearted pop-up singing and social-media-organized riot, or revenge porn which might well be simulated through an app[20] – all play with the idea that there might be a sight that alters your real-world life for ever, even as they push the possibility away as threatening the mixed real/not-real form.

Modern tourism plays a parallel game in the 'real world' with carefully curated and bounded locations which are set up to signify different kinds of extremity, historical, visual and experiential, promising limited engagement that will 'feel real' and yet remain entertainment rather than encounter – a tricky balance to achieve. And charity advertising constantly struggles with the question of how to persuade people deadened by scopophilia to venture any genuine empathic relationship with the human beings in need whose semi-fictionalized images they are pressed

---

20 See www.vice.com/en_uk/article/kzm59x/deepnude-app-creates-fake-nudes-of-any-woman (accessed 09.01.2020).

to feel things about – particularly as the object of the exercise is not sympathy but money. How may such advertising balance need, tragedy or oppression against hope, endeavour and possibility? Staging and audience manipulation go with the territory.

And then there is the viewing of sexualized images of children. No guarantee of unreality, however complete, could define such looking as harmless. In interviews conducted within a research study, offenders characterized the internet both as a safely anonymous place to express a hidden or unknown self – 'The internet is a sort of means for pretending you're something you're not'[21] – and as a place that is no-place and in which nothing really happens – 'You know, you're on the internet, you can't hurt anyone, it's not wrong . . . I'm not doing any more hurt by viewing them.'[22] But such opinions, common to almost any other kind of looking, have no weight here. Looking is doing. The interviewees themselves know that. One located all his feelings in the physical machine of the computer, hoping they might be left behind there, safely unreal: 'Once I had left the place of, you know, I just, it just wasn't with me any more . . . it was a shutting, the machine would be shut down.' But it didn't work. He added, 'I felt sick every time I did it though.'[23]

As Jesus remarked, the evil done by looking is an evil of intention. Those who examine illegal images as part of an investigative police process are not defined as evil, though I wonder how much defence anyone has against the toxic nature of the material. Intentions, though, are not always easy to assess, even perhaps for the mind and heart of the person having them; nor is it always easy to distinguish intentions from desires and

---

21 Ethel Quayle et al., *Online Behaviour Related to Child Sexual Abuse* (Council of the Baltic Sea States, 2012), www.innocenceindanger. de/wp-content/uploads/2014/05/Interviews_online_offenders.pdf, p. 37. Uploaded from the Lucy Faithfull Foundation website (accessed 09.01.2020).

22 *Online Behaviour*, p. 51.

23 *Online Behaviour*, p. 35.

feelings.[24] The rise in crimes of this kind seems to be linked with nudge algorithms, which allow the watcher to slide from 'mainstream' 'teen' or 'school' fantasies to content that moves down the age-range bit by bit so that the point of fall may be difficult to locate. Add to this the practice of 'normalization' making the world of porn comfortable to navigate, and it becomes clear that a watcher can feel supportively accompanied all the way to a terrible place. Add again the general tendency to see online interactions as closer to the privacy of thought than to action, the wish for a sense of intensity associated with transgressing boundaries, and the assumption that watching anything doesn't alter the essential self, and all the conditions are perfectly set for large numbers of people whose psychic fractures may in fact not match absolutely perfectly on to this particular transgression, but for whom the fit is 'good enough', to find themselves in a hell they had not quite planned to visit.

In an attempt to stamp out the child porn industry by taking out its customers (a technique trialled in the 'war on drugs', where it hasn't worked either), some forms of recent police rhetoric exactly equate watching child porn to active real-world abuse. This equation assumes that every image has a real child behind it, which, though not absolutely true given all the faking possibilities available, is probably true enough to have weight. But the *intention* behind such viewing will be decidedly different between the active real-world seeking out of real-world children (including via chatrooms) and the passive watching of images that may feel as if they are at least partly a form of inner thought or even memory.[25]

Sentencing policy has to consider this difference of intention, a difference that gives some indication of whether contact

24 See Anne Richards, 'Nakedness and Vulnerability', in *Through the Eyes of a Child*, ed. A. Richards and P. Privett (London: Church House Publishing, 2018).

25 M. Glasser, I. Kolvin et al., 'Cycle of child sexual abuse: Links between being a victim and becoming a perpetrator', *The British Journal of Psychiatry* 179:6 (December 2001), pp. 482–94. Available from www.kolvinpsych.net/sites/default/files/pdf/cycle-of-child-sexual-abuse-links-between-being-a-victim-and-becoming-a-perpetrator.pdf (accessed 09.01.2020).

offence might be likely, because the sheer and growing numbers of people convicted of child porn offences are stretching police capacity. At least one thoughtful senior policeman, Simon Bailey, the National Police Chiefs' Council lead on child protection, has, controversially, challenged the rhetoric's logic as well as its doability.[26] Leaving aside the extremely unsettled argument between different experts about how many 'non-contact' watchers go on to abuse children, he points out that nudge algorithms are there to send people over the line from 'mainstream' to abusive viewing, something that could be tackled by requiring big tech to change its practices.[27]

Everyone knows that the watcher of child porn will forever be defined by what he has done. That he has never been like anyone else and cannot become better. That for all civic purposes he should be the living dead. He should not be employed, he should not live anywhere in particular, he should not have friends or family. He is a social outcast, a goat carrying the scopophilic sins of a whole society into the wilderness. This is how we try to expunge the impure in order to guarantee the purity of everyone else. It doesn't work. In fact it makes it harder to tackle the problem. The line between legal pornography that *imagines* raping schoolchildren ('Teen Punishment') and the uncontroversially illegal image is not as clear as people want it to be. We find the popular characterization of the barely human paedophile necessary because our society is uncertain, except in this one instance, about what constitutes evil and abusive looking. It is like the way 1990s drug-heavy, opiate-heavy rave culture got very sniffy about heroin users because its do-what-you-like ethic suddenly needed to have a fierce, absolutely solid invisible clause in order for the ethic to survive. Do what you like, do anything you like, *but not this*.

---

26 See www.theguardian.com/uk-news/2014/dec/05/top-police-officer-many-viewing-child-abuse-images-treated-nhs; www.independent.co.uk/news/uk/crime/child-sex-abuse-paedophile-police-images-a8902036.html (both accessed 10.01.2020).

27 See www.edp24.co.uk/news/crime/norfolk-chief-constable-simon-bailey-calls-for-social-media-boycott-1-6044607 (accessed 10.01.2020).

The secrets of the heart

Writing about 'Looking' has taken me to places I really didn't want to visit, and turned out to be more important than I first understood. It's been straightforward to argue that looking is at the centre of the cultural changes brought about by the techno-logical revolution of the last 20 years, because screens have so far been the main means for the rise of tech, and screens require you to look at a flat surface and imagine it to be 3-dimensional. The larger argument is less susceptible to proof: that a culture of continual watchers brings particular fears, anxieties and hopes to their watching habits, especially when they fear – or hope – that there is no God to keep them in his eye. I can't prove it, I can only propose it as a thought-experiment, and I propose it from the point of view of someone for whom God's eye is fundamentally steadying, fully steadfast.

So now I am going to take it to its logical end, knowing that for many it can't be anything but a thought-experiment. When Paul wrote to the people of Corinth, he described the future joy of encountering the presence of God like this: 'For now we see in a mirror, dimly, but then we will see face to face. Now I know only in part; then I will know fully, even as I have been fully known.'[28] Behind all the desires for connection is the desire to be 'fully known'. The idea is terrifying but it has such power – that every thought, every moment, from the most shameful wish to the unregarded virtue of some inner victory, might all be *realized*, exposed to the clear light of morning so that you become released from the shame, and sustained by the victories no one else knew. Those seem to be the impulses gov-erning much modern communication, though they also don't seem to be working very well.

In the course of Jon Ronson's investigations, he got into an email correspondence with a gay porn star, Connor Habib, about the nature of shame, a discussion that arose out of Ronson's curiosity about how Habib coped with the internet displaying explicit images of his anus. Habib talked about how

---

28 1 Corinthians 13.12.

much people might have to learn from porn actors about the stripped-down self that can be found beyond self-exposure. He went on to say that a lot of sex industry workers go on to become hospice workers: 'They're not freaked out by the body, so they can help people transition through illness and death. I'm not sure what would humiliate me at this point.'[29] As Habib describes it, the experience of being on the receiving end of a mass of different projections by a mass of different anonymous men can give you the strength and charity to help others to face the exposure and humiliations of the dying process.

'Nothing is hidden that will not be disclosed,' said Jesus to his companions after telling the story of the sower, 'nor is anything secret that will not become known and come to light. Then pay attention [the Greek word is *blepete*, or 'see'] to how you listen; for to those who have, more shall be given; and from those who do not have, even what they seem to have will be taken away.'[30]

Is that a threat? I think it is a remark about how things are. It is a warning about learning to look with a clear eye. The phrase 'what you seem to have' includes the Greek verb, *dokeō*; another way of translating the phrase is 'what you *think* you have', and the word *dokeō* itself hints that this might be an unreliable, subjective judgement. Jesus is asking whether you are sure that what you think you possess is either really there or has the value you think it has. Because if it's not really there, or means something else, it's no good to you. He is saying something about masks, and personae, and the point where those ghosts abandon you and leave you with the truth of the stripped-down self. And, he says, the stuff that's really there is not what's on the outside, not whether you kept within the law or had people's respect or managed to control your expression of the bad stuff, but what's on the inside projecting out. Some of it is good, and some of it is shameful; but when it is exposed to the light of the divine gaze, when you are 'fully known', no malign ghost of shame or transgression can ever again have the power to hurt you.

---

29 Ronson, *Shamed*, p. 141.
30 Luke 8.17–18.

4

Joining

1 MEMORY

Sex education

under the bramble bushes
under the sea   boom boom boom
true love for you my darling
true love for me
and we'll get married
and raise a family   and so it's
under the bramble bushes
under the sea   boom boom boom
Esso Blue means happy motoring
Esso Blue means happy motoring
Esso Blue means happy motoring
Es   -   so   -   Blue![1]

This clapping rhyme was popular across the 1960s and 1970s. The version here is the one I knew at primary school, which had somehow got a 1950s advert for petrol tacked on to it. Its adventurous beginning, borrowed from Edwardian music hall, gives way to the suburban marriage dream: true love, mum, dad, and the 2.5 babies, all motoring together in the family car. I could see them in my mind's eye as we clapped, driving past huge, storm-driven clumps of brambles towards a day at the

---

1 See www.bl.uk/collection-items/under-the-bram-brush (accessed 10.01.2020).

coast – though I always had a feeling that they ought also to drive off a cliff into the sea, in vague association with the film *Chitty Chitty Bang Bang*.

The primary school I went to, like the clapping rhyme, mixed the Edwardian past with undigested modern innovation. It had, and used, the cane. And it banned rote-learning as deadening for the young mind. One teacher defied the ban on times tables (she posted sentries and had us whisper them to her before assembly) or I would even now be struggling with 7x8. As an early reader – once I finally found a way to persuade teachers who punished answering-back that I actually could read – I was grudgingly given the new, brightly coloured multi-ethnic reading books while slower, often bilingual first-generation Sicilian, Neapolitan or Kashmiri readers toiled through months of 'look and say' with Peter and Jane.[2]

The really destabilizing thing about school was that its management was hugely anxious about 'elitism', but still used the mechanisms of competition, so it was never clear whether hard work would be rewarded or irritably dismissed. I learnt the hard way that I was supposed to enjoy dancing to 'Bridge over Troubled Water' in 'music and movement' classes more than learning 'Nymphs and Shepherds, come away' from the defiantly old-fashioned music teacher.[3] I was not a natural dancer. Winning the handwriting prize and spelling tests courted social disaster – with the teachers. Like most girls, when it came to trying to please I was not easy to de-programme, though I did

---

2 The 'Peter and Jane' series of children's reading books, first published by Ladybird in 1964, feature a 1950s-style, middle-class white suburban couple of children in a markedly gender-stereotyped nuclear family, and their dog, Pat. They formed part of a fashionable reading experiment that relied solely on repeated word recognition.

3 'Nymphs and Shepherds, come away', by Henry Purcell, was the piece chosen for an influential musical experiment in Manchester in 1929, which introduced local schoolchildren to singing classical music. 'Bridge over Troubled Water', a gospel-influenced song by Paul Simon and Art Garfunkel from 1970, features in *Rolling Stone*'s '500 best songs of all time'. We did not learn to sing it.

become bewildered, disaffected and, by the time I was 11, downright miserable.

The playground was run on much clearer lines. Boys occupied it. All of it. They played football and war games from the centre to the periphery, playing out their own versions of World War Two and the frontier wars of America. (I am not sure how gentle boys coped, though significantly none of my brothers enjoyed school and all of them spent many years making their own personal accommodations with machismo.) Girls hung on in a narrow band round the edge, playing clapping games that sang about love and marriage, skipping games that sang about love and marriage, or hanging dangerously from the bars of the concrete steps talking about, well, love and marriage. Girls did not play football and boys did not skip or clap. Conversation between boys and girls was conducted entirely in terms of shouted insult. There were only two games that everyone played together, 'British Bulldog', which at its whirlwind climax involved huge linked lines of children running other children down in ones and twos, and 'Kiss chase', which involved boys catching girls, pinning them to the fence by their hands and kissing them.

Kiss chase had its own complexities. It sounds simple, but in fact there were subtle rules about how fast you ran, and about how often and how quickly you allowed yourself to be caught. Linger too much and you were 'easy'; run too fast and you were cheating. Struggling was required but should not be successful. You turned your face away from the kiss but you did not refuse it. You should not be caught too often, but just often enough. These subtleties were not easy to get right. Kiss chase was a game that socialized children for later roles in which, although men would be pursuers and women the pursued, women must be quietly complicit in their own capture, which should not be too swift or obvious or they would be 'cheapened'. Nothing should look mutual. The game itself must be played assuming that only women cared about love and bargained reluctant men – who would rather get on with sterner stuff – into the marriage-trap with baits of hard-won kisses.

The world was changing very rapidly then. By the time I got to my teens, courting conventions were in disarray, with the marriage-threat (fairly) distant for both sexes, contraception grudgingly available if you could stand the shame (I never met a boy who would admit to being willing to use a condom, or who ever carried any, whatever his intentions), and the 1970s' discourse of 'free love' everywhere you looked. But underneath the froth, the rules governing male/female encounter were exactly the same at 16 as they had been at 6 – just much, much harder to negotiate. The deal was no longer explicit. The terms under which you could say no had spectacularly diminished, the social punishment for saying yes (if a girl) as huge as ever it had been in earlier generations. Not just a possible baby, but widespread, jeering, masculine contempt.

The most recognizable description I have ever come across of my suburban teenage years appears in Nick Hornby's early novel *High Fidelity*. His narrator, geekily obsessed with the minutiae of rare records and maker of endless lists and cassette 'variouses' – I knew many versions of him – writes eloquently about sexual experiment from a male point of view in terms of the slow frustrations of colonization. 'It was as if breasts were little pieces of property that had been unlawfully annexed by the opposite sex – they were rightfully ours and we wanted them back.' This is not an isolated observation. The singer Robyn Hitchcock had a more lonely and sinister take on the same theme. In his song 'Sometimes I wish I was a pretty girl', Hitchcock fantasizes that he would then have a woman available to attack – himself – 'in the show-*er*!'[4] I didn't then get the *Psycho* reference but the song bothered me. Home was full of boys, friends of my younger brothers, who thought the lines hilarious, and sang along loudly from the next-door bedroom.

I see bits of myself, painfully, in the second girlfriend appearing in the Hornby novel, Penny Hardwick, the posh nice girl

---

4 Robyn Hitchcock and the Egyptians (surrealist singer/songwriter and former member of the Soft Boys), 'Sometimes I wish I was a pretty girl', on *I Often Dream of Trains* (1984). See www.youtube.com/watch?v=WdJ9ZSt3f_0 (accessed 10.01.2020).

with the lovely parents. During the narrator's last encounter with her, the one where he decides he is never going to 'get any' and there's therefore no point in going on with the relationship, he 'used a degree of force that would have outraged and terrified an adult female, but got nowhere, and when I walked her home we hardly spoke'.[5] Later he is astonished to find her conceding everything shortly afterwards to a confident rival in an encounter that she herself describes, years later, as 'that little shitbag asked me out, and I was too tired to fight him off'.

The extent to which a 1970s' adolescence, for a suburban girl, was a war of attrition from puberty onwards, is difficult to overstate. (The war was not confined to my own age group: adult men, including those in positions of trust, were an accepted hazard of life. You couldn't report such men, only outwit them – if you were lucky. I was mostly lucky, though it was a close thing a couple of times. Some of my friends were not.) My happiest summer was spent with a stunningly beautiful, self-consciously manly older boy who went everywhere with me, took me to Led Zeppelin at Knebworth on the bus, introduced me to his mum and dad, and walked with me on a pilgrimage from Winchester to Canterbury. With hindsight, I now understand that the glory of that 1979 summer was because he was gay. I will have been in part a cover story for a differently difficult time. All I noticed then was that he actually seemed to want to be friends.

As with school, I spent anxious hours trying to learn the rules; as with school, it seemed the sets of rules to learn were so incompatible that failure could be the only outcome. (Ignoring, or opposing, others' impossible rules did not occur to me then, and only gradually later.) The dilemma of that time was this. One set of expectations placed enormous value on sexual activity as *gift*, to be offered in an undefended way, no strings, for the transcendent joy of the moment; but another (held by exactly the same people) participated wholeheartedly in the old-fashioned whore/madonna divisions of previous generations. Add to this the fairly astonishing assumption

---

5 Nick Hornby, *High Fidelity* (London: Penguin, 2014), pp. 7, 9, 133.

that when girls held back it was because they wanted to trick or lure young men into marriage and responsibility (it never seemed to occur to anyone that *girls* might have reasons to avoid marriage) and the lengthening of adolescence into what all previous generations would have seen as full adult life, and you had an impossible mix of tensions to manage.[6]

I did not know what to do. I was – perhaps excessively – horrified by the idea of manipulating anyone into commitment, which was always assumed to be the motive behind refusing to go 'all the way'. This hurt my pride. The idea of transcendent gift, and hang the cost, was very attractive. It chimed with the mad generosity I recognized in Christian living. But undefended sexual gift didn't seem to work out so well in books; I had read a lot of Thomas Hardy by then and could see considerable downsides. Playing up the madonna aspect of things seemed the only defence, and I knew it to be fatally flimsy. Asking my doctor to help was unimaginable. It was only a matter of time. Gloomily, I got a copy of *The L-Shaped Room* out of the library and hoped for the best.[7]

I had read *The Screwtape Letters*. I knew, therefore, that every sexual encounter sets up a 'transcendental relation' which must be 'eternally enjoyed or eternally endured'.[8] This seemed daunting in the circumstances. I still don't know whether I perhaps believe it; it bit very deep. Aged 14, and disappointed in love, I had discovered my local Anglican church, then in the grip of the 1970s' charismatic revival. I owe that church, and its youth club, a lot; it gave me a whole structure for faith on which I know I still rely, carefully grounded

6 My friend, marrying in her teens (it didn't last), had Godley and Creme's 1981 hit 'Wedding Bells' dedicated to her by the DJ at the reception. Perhaps he was misled by the title, or perhaps he was having a laugh. The song's viewpoint is of a reluctant man who wants sex but resents his girlfriend's attempts to make it conditional on marrying her.

7 *The L-Shaped Room*, by Lynne Reid Banks (London: Chatto and Windus, 1960), is a bestselling novel (and latterly a film) about being an unmarried mother in a bleak bedsit.

8 C. S. Lewis, *The Screwtape Letters* (London: Harper Collins, 2012 [1942]), p. 66.

and balanced in ways that the charismatic house church I also briefly attended was decidedly not. But the expectations of evangelical-charismatic culture added a new layer of complexity. Gerald Coates' youth weekends away had stern things to say about virginity and saving yourself for marriage, nothing to say about contraception.

That house church. It was definitely *not* Anglican: it had broken from the local charismatic Baptists in a row over faith healing. I wasn't always sure what I was seeing, but I knew enough to recognize the sexual component in the proto-orgasmic fits that accompanied 'speaking in tongues', especially for the vulnerable older women involved. (They were probably about 35, and all on the rebound from failed relationships.) I also saw the drive to absolute power animating the church's founders. They were the only ones allowed to 'interpret' tongues, and they bullied those unhappy women unmercifully with their 'interpretations'. They had a nose for the mildest, most tentative flirting. They attempted to force me into ecstatic conformity at a charismatic 'healing meeting' in Byfleet Village Hall, announcing that I was possessed by a 'liturgical spirit' and must be exorcised. The exorcism failed (evidently) but was so terrifying I can only remember a few flashingly disjunctive images. One is of a punk couple – safety pins, piercings, green mohican, tartan and leather, the lot – peeping through the door and withdrawing swiftly, and my sense that with them sanity and potential rescue had withdrawn too. I still shrink from being physically leaned over in prayer. I didn't go back.

What the house church leaders saw, and took steps over, was my reluctance to enter an undefended state of ecstasy. The 'liturgical spirit' they identified got in the way, as they saw it, of the Spirit's moving. They were quite right that I was suspicious of that particular meeting – full of people obviously *pretending* to be healed – but wrong in general. The joys of ecstasy were mine. I danced under the strobe to 'Silver Machine'.[9] I flew along the bypass on the backs of real Triumphs and Harley

9 Hawkwind, 'Silver Machine' (1971), an electronic paean to motorbikes, with wind machine.

Davidsons. I sang in tongues in Christ Church, Woking, the same five notes repeating and repeating at different times, curling like smoke across the high roof of the building. I played the unpredictable real-time improvisations of Terry Riley's 'In C' with the Surrey Wind Orchestra.[10] All these were variants of the same intense, fluid, antinomian delight. The only place where I could not afford to feel it was in the relentless and exhausting battles over sex.

Pretty soon my unplanned pregnancy liberated me, whether I liked it or not, from the whole world of evangelical youth Christianity. I left it behind with a kind of relief. When I got to university, a single mother of 19 with a 10-month-old, I spent the first two terms watching my contemporaries and trying to work out who was exploiting whom. I had not really seen civility between the sexes before, nor had I been in a society that allowed men and women to be openly gay. Although I had lost all the freedom of my youth, and although what lay ahead was years of unceasing toil, trying to recoup something I would have had on much easier terms had I handled my adolescence better, I still felt that I had come from a stifling prison to a much more kindly open space. It was a while before I got up the courage to go back to church.

Aftermath

I've talked about this for several reasons. This is the world that made me. It's not the only influence, and it's quite a long way down the geological layers now, but in telling it I show what went into the person who is doing her thinking about sexuality. I am not some objective assessing eye, of the kind gallantly

---

10 Terry Riley's 1964 composition 'In C' provides different members of an ensemble with short phrases in the key of C, which are then combined by the conductor in any order during performance. It formed an influential part of the minimalist and experimental wing of classical music during the 1960s and 1970s. The result sounds quite like singing in tongues, but louder.

aimed at in the various national church bodies on 'human sexuality' of which I have been part. It has, at times, felt completely ridiculous to pretend to be such an eye – and I also notice that as a heterosexual I have been treated as strangely unproblematic in spite of my history, and allowed quite a bit more privacy than non-straight colleagues. I am grateful for the courtesy, but it is unfair. I am a player, not an observer, in a field of extraordinary complexity. It seems necessary to show what has gone into both my bias and my insight.

And, of course, I have left a lot out. There were real relationships with people which contained real tenderness, real conversation, shared experience and pleasure. I enjoyed the company of young men – I grew up in a household of boys, after all. And human relationships and recognitions find ways round even the most toxic of systems. All that belongs to a private life that has no place here. There are other, difficult memories, memories to which I would not return for any reason at all and certainly not in public, which sit between myself and my God, subject both to his judgement and, I trust, his mercy. They also have no place here.

I wasn't a good subject for the 1970s moment. I was hopelessly literal-minded. I spent pointless hours pursuing the logic of assumptions that probably had none, at any rate for the person making them. I believed everything I read. More pragmatic, braver, less anxiously compliant female contemporaries managed better.

But I do not in fact believe that the world that made me was only locally toxic or that its effects are really dissipated.[11] Unless leafy Surrey in 1981 was uniquely afflicted with satyriasis, which doesn't seem likely, then the many 50-somethings running the Church, and indeed the country, grew up in variants of that world: some gentler, some much worse. Yesterday

---

11 The data discussed in Caroline Criado-Perez's book *Invisible Women: Exposing Data Bias in a World Designed for Men* (London: Chatto and Windus, 2019), particularly the data dealing with silencing, sexual harassment, sexual assault, and the socialization of girls, suggests far less has changed since the 1970s than I hoped. See, for example, the chapter 'Gender Neutral with Urinals' (pp. 47–66), where a number of these issues are considered in the context of daily life.

sits under today inflecting its meanings, either in conformity or in contrast: that is why we need historians.

So I make no apology for a chapter that sets the patterns of memory behind the method of its thinking. I write as some-one thinking over what she sees from the perspective she has. That perspective doesn't fit completely neatly with either of the competing narratives around which the Church's arguments over sex are locked, and it's at a slightly odd angle to secular liberal orthodoxies as well. But then, I wonder how well all those narratives are serving us.

So here are a couple of different maps of what I understand, from that perspective: a map of social change around sex, and a map of different ecclesial responses, especially within the Church of England, to that change. They are partial, illustra-tive, speculative. I hope they will also look familiar.

2 MAPS

Social moralities, personal permissions

Between the 1960s and the 1990s society changed. Sexual activity appeared to shift from being a moralized, consequence-laden aspect of public behaviour tied into the social institutions of marriage and family, to being a private, implicitly neutral choice. But this isn't the whole truth, and of course the change happened jerkily, in bits, with other assumptions taking a bit of time to catch up.

Marriage and family did not disappear. Instead the shapes of family responsibility altered. More informal, often temporary cohabitations emerged alongside marriage, and divorce rates among the married shot up.[1] Meanwhile, redefining sex as a private choice created different moral dilemmas, clustering around issues of consent, social and personal responsibility, and what constituted sexual harm. For a while opinions on those issues were in disarray.

The informal contract between men and women that had existed before – implied in the girls' custodianship of 'love and marriage' at the edge of the playground while the boys occupied its centre and played at war – was seriously disrupted. Before sex split away from family responsibility women had been unacknowledged guardians of the shift towards adult burdens, the social brakes on male excess. The seven children borne by my maternal grandmother thrived because my grandfather handed over his wages for the housekeeping and did not drink. He had a say – he intervened when my grandmother wanted to refuse my mother's grammar school place because of the cost of the uniform, as her own mother had done to her – but his authority was held inside an informally matriarchal regulation of behaviour. Such female influence could only be indirect; it could not be enforced. But it was powerful, and therefore it fuelled resentment as well as respect.

---

1 See www.theguardian.com/news/datablog/2010/jan/28/divorce-rates-marriage-ons (accessed 10.01.2020).

When the 1970s changed the rules about sex, those social brakes came off. For a while men, astonished at the change, behaved like greedy schoolboys in an unguarded sweet shop. The men and boys around in my growing up still believed it was a kind of trick, though; women were pretending to go along but really, underneath, they planned to betray them into adult responsibility – and they could see in the world around them that lots of people weren't having to settle for that. So men demanded sex they weren't sure they would be granted, despised the women and girls who were prepared to offer it, because, well, they were sluts, weren't they? – and prepared to fight for their freedoms if things went wrong.

For initially this new world of more sexual freedom, with sexual activity partly separated from social roles and responsibilities, emerged into a society in which women, the young and the vulnerable still had little say in what happened to their bodies. Women had lost the social control they had once had; family and responsibility had lost their dignity and their weight, and what had once been a balance of power tipped over. Impulse, 'spontaneity' and recklessness acquired huge cultural value. People got hurt, but the message was that acting on impulse was always worth it; only the repressively mean-spirited would ever complain.

Over the course of four more decades the world shifted again. When the powerful acted on impulse people didn't always feel they had to comply. Sexual decisions started to require negotiation. This is being a slow and partial process, as evidenced by the #MeToo movement and the many sexual abuse scandals coming to light, within and outside church structures.

Reliable contraception made a huge change to people's lives, especially in the form of the contraceptive pill, which could truly be controlled by women. This made it possible to define sexual activity as a private pleasure. Indeed, because of contraception, it became much more possible to reassign childbearing as just a minor part of 'being a woman'. Contraception eased, but also made more necessary, the public rise of feminism, in a context where the first fine careless rapture of 'liberation' was not noted for its masculine impulse control. And, of course, contraception made it possible for women to try out the heady experience of consequence-less action themselves. Through contraception and its consequences it also became possible for women to take a much fuller part in economic and public life.

Although the benefits of contraception passed me by in my teens, I benefited from the social change it brought throughout the rest of my adult life. Without it, I would never have been able to be a full part of any of the different professional worlds I later occupied, or use the abilities with which I was born.

Yet the weakened link between sex and responsibility, the way men and women could change their minds about what satisfied them, and the assumption that everyone should be sexually active, had another consequence. Women and children would disproportionately bear the impact of the search for fulfilment. Women's continuing responsibility for childbearing, the vast majority of child-nurture, and family caring of other kinds, faded from public view as it became less socially defining of what a woman either was, or did.[2] Single-parent families proliferated, mostly headed by women – today one-fifth of the UK's children are growing up with one parent and 90 per cent of those single parents are mothers.[3] I knew that world, too; Mrs Thatcher's 'feckless single parents' rang in our ears as I and my older daughter made a household together. The hungriest we have ever been was in the structurally punishing shift from welfare benefits to paid work, when I started teaching piecemeal for the Open University. (And we had a *lot* of social capital.)

Little has changed, though policy decisions around family shape and its economics have risen and fallen like the sea. Welfare benefits changes, the rise of zero-hours contracts and patterns of ill-paid part-time work have all assisted in keeping

---

2 For the data behind this assertion, see Caroline Criado Perez, 'The Long Friday', in *Invisible Women: Exposing Data Bias in a World Designed for Men* (London: Chatto and Windus, 2019), pp. 69–91.

3 Office of National Statistics, 'Families and Households: 2018'. The figure is 21.1 per cent. See also www.gingerbread.org.uk/what-we-do/media-centre/single-parents-facts-figures/ (accessed 10.01.2020).

single-parent households poor.[4] Yet the apparently broken link between sex and childbearing makes it much less easy to see the impact that childbearing still has on women's lives.

With sex separable from making babies, what 'counted' as sexual activity also subtly altered. In the days when sex and babies were linked, you could say that the kinds of sexual encounter that might result in a baby *were* 'sex'. All other activity that involved penile penetration also counted as 'sex' – perhaps because it was analogous to what you had to do to make babies. It is really striking (though not perhaps surprising, given the widespread use of rape as both a domestic and a political weapon) the extent to which arguments over 'sex' have tended to be arguments about where those who possess penises should, or should not, put them.

Yet the effect of this focus on penile penetrative activity was that almost every other kind of sexualized touching or stimulation could be called something else. Bill Clinton (during the Monica Lewinski scandal) is the most notorious heterosexual to try out conveniently narrow definitions of 'sex'; but Anglo-Catholic male, clerical gay culture of the time also found it helpful to keep 'sex' narrowly defined as a sacralized mechanism for baby-making, allowing as it did for a homosocial world of physical intimacy that could quietly flourish under some other heading. The very different worlds of sexual abuse ('I'm not abusing him/her, this is just touching and does no harm') and that of casuistical 'rule-keeping' ('yes, we are saving ourselves for marriage, this is just a bit of harmless exploration') were some other contrasting contexts profiting from narrow definitions of the erotic.[5]

---

4 Martin Culliney, Tina Haux and Stephen McKay, 'Family Structure and Poverty in the UK', April 2014 (supported by the Joseph Rowntree Foundation). Available from http://eprints.lincoln.ac.uk/14958/1/Family_structure_report_Lincoln.pdf (accessed 10.01.2020).

5 Rachel Mann, among others, comments on this: www.therachelmannblogspot.blogspot.com, 'The Limits of Sex', 6 September 2018. See also Helen King, https://sharedconversations.wordpress.com/2016/01/20/what-is-sex-anyway/ (both accessed 10.01.2020).

Meanwhile, along with other changes in reproductive technology, contraception helped to emphasize similarities, rather than differences, between same-sex and heterosexual couples, and, in the wake of the rise of feminism, to make it possible to imagine more flexible gender roles. What women did together sexually, penis-free though it was, began to acquire some visibility outside the desirous male gaze.[6] Space also emerged for gay men and women to begin to explore visible social roles as couples and households, which had formerly been exclusive to heterosexuals. The old battles between men and women about how responsibilities should be allocated in households began to be influenced by different, less gendered patterns of shared life; the old certainties and resentments began to be informed by different visions of human relationship.

But the road to general acceptance was not smooth. The row leading to 'Section 28', the 1988 British legislation that forbade the 'intentional promotion' by local authorities of homosexuality, was triggered by a *Daily Mail* article about a children's book stocked by a primary school, *Jenny Lives with Eric and Martin*, exploring a model of family with two gay male parents.[7] Although what men did together privately was the prurient background to the *Mail*'s interest (especially at the height of public anxiety generated by the AIDS epidemic), what made it a story was two things: that the book suggested same-sex relationships happened in conventional domestic settings, and that children should be told so in school. The grounds for objection were that the book promoted the 'unnatural'; but what was really revolutionary about it was the ordering of a gay household within such a traditional frame. Parents caring for a child in a nuclear family? So far, so ordinary. But one where a girl child was being cared for by two men? Bizarre. What could be weirder than such a gender role switch?

---

6 That said, 'Lesbian' inhabits the top search term spot by volume in Pornhub's 2018 analytics, and comes up high (fourth) in the 'most viewed' category for male watchers.

7 See https://en.wikipedia.org/wiki/Section_28 (accessed 10.01.2020).

Invitation, harassment, social anxiety and threat

Over time, people have become much less narrow about what counts as sexual encounter. But the blurry line this creates between 'sex' and other kinds of intimacy has its own problems. The erotic has become more dissipated yet more subtly constant, even threatening. Several decades of culturally sanctioned poor impulse control has created anxieties about how feelings with sexual potential may be expressed acceptably. There is much more emphasis put on discerning the *intentions* behind certain kinds of touching, looking or talking in the judgements people make about what constitutes 'appropriate' interaction.

Intentions are hard to read from the outside – and can be misread. Their signs can be brief, ambiguous. The suspicious eye spreads suspicion, not safety; yet it is prudent to be wary. No regrets for access-all-areas masculine greed, but – insofar as it *has* departed from civil interaction – its memory has narrowed the exploratory space for mutuality. We approach each other through tentative negotiation in potentially hostile territory.

Sexual encounter is governed by two simple principles: do no harm, and establish mutual consent. These are, of course, absolutely necessary preconditions, but they are being required to carry a lot of weight in the absence of any more widely accepted sexual ethic. 'Do no harm' is not a straightforward principle to apply – not all harm is immediately visible. Mutual consent is complex to establish and the relative power of each person alters the nature of its supposed mutuality. On their own, these principles are vital rather than adequate to the job of regulation.

It is possible for one person to see harassment where another was only aware of friendly encounter, or for very different understandings of consent to collide, before or after the fact. How words are phrased may matter as much as who touches whom and where on the body the touching happens. Stories and jokes about sex can be heard from very different moral standpoints. Consider, for example, 'Donglegate', the corny penis joke between two men overheard by a woman at a 2013 tech conference to which she took public offence; the

subsequent Twitter storm for and against her outrage lost the
male joke-teller and ultimately the woman herself their jobs.[8]
Touching itself has become an extremely charged and anxious
activity, particularly in contexts where one person has visibly
more social power than another. Distance is often seen to be
safer than a mis-readable friendly intimacy.

Encounters that are pre-defined as 'dating', with a set of
boundaries already mutually agreed (as with online dating
apps), can feel a much safer, more regulated route than the
wilder, less mutually agreed places of non-virtual social encounter. Workplaces, once a prime social space for courtship, are
particularly fraught, because they are usually hierarchies, so that
power imbalance is an instant problem. HR managers discour-
age workplace relationships. The social rules governing consent and harassment are complex and not entirely stable. Their
nuances, and the boundaries of erotic encounter, are intimately
tied into the play of different kinds of social power and social
vulnerability: of influence and agency, gender, identity, beauty,
youth, seniority, money, race, class. Because these are in com-
petitive flux it is not always clear what is, and what is not, okay.

Yet, at the same time as the number of voices competing
for the right to be heard has multiplied, the routes by which
offence is judged has, through social media, become more collective, less rule-bound and more arbitrary. Legal redress for
rape, assault and domestic abuse is as clogged and slow as ever
it was, unequal between rich and poor because of inequalities
of access to legal assistance, and bruisingly adversarial. But
for symbolic personal infringements, the punishment is public, swift, notably unhampered by any regulated judgement
process, involving extreme threats and fantasies in which the
sexual mixes promiscuously with the violent. Women are
particularly targeted. No one is immune.

---

8 Jon Ronson, *So You've Been Publicly Shamed* (London: Picador,
2015), pp. 105–25. Although online-fuelled punishment fell on both
parties, the man found a job within a week, in an all-male office. The
woman was out of work for over a year and received extreme physical
and sexual threats online.

The civil war over sex

All parts of society, from government and lawmakers down to much more local levels, have been deeply involved in meeting the challenges of sexual privatization, but religious organizations have regarded it with that special urgency that goes with anxiety about what it might mean for their own survival.

In the Church of England, competing accounts of religion's place in this meta-story slug it out endlessly. There is a progressive version where the world shakes off the chains of prejudice, conformity and stultified gender roles, establishing an essentially sacred change for the better with which the stuffy old Church must catch up. In this version the gendered constraints and hypocrisies of the pre-permissive world are exposed as a spent violence. The Church should embrace change, ushering in a renewed, more generous and more mutual relationship between faith and the secular world. It should hallow a wider range of sexual relationships than the current offering of monogamous, heterosexual marriage. Along with this would go (though this bit is talked about less than you would imagine) the tolerance of a wide range of relationships/sexual encounters before marriage, or between marriages for those whose marriages have failed, as part of the search for a viable long-term hallowed relationship that works. Nadia Bolz-Weber has recently told an American Lutheran version of this narrative with considerable eloquence and with more honesty than is usual for the Church of England version, but set in a different world, a world where religion has unimaginably more clout than in the UK. But we have UK versions too.[9]

Other storytellers offer a more nostalgic account. Once upon a time, they say, people knew the meanings of commitment and self-control but have now forgotten them, to society's spiritual detriment. In this version, the Church is also gradually forgetting the importance of commitment, the sacredness of marriage,

---

9 Nadia Bolz-Weber, *Shameless* (Norwich: Canterbury Press, 2019); Jonathan Bartley, *Faith and Politics after Christendom* (Milton Keynes: Paternoster Press, 2006).

the virtue of sexual continence, true family values that put the nurture of children at the centre, the need to re-establish neater, more complementary ways of understanding right relationships between men and women. The Church's readiness to forget its moral roots is dangerous, not least because it collapses the boundary between the ethics of Church and world and therefore courts the already clear and present danger of rendering the Church redundant. Some of these accounts theologize their nostalgia in the light of a strikingly unitary reading of the Bible. For them, the patriarchal nuclear marriage values of the post-industrial West are God's primary channel for teaching his creatures about the divine–human relationship.

Each of these competing accounts strikes me as synthetic, polemical and highly selective. (Or, to put it more directly, untrue.) The 'progressive' version doesn't consider the cultural pressure upon individuals to be sexually active and successful, or the anxiety that builds around the constant presence of the erotic as a commodity, even as sexual permission takes other kinds of pressure off. It seems bound to a vision of 'progress' that doesn't seem entirely borne out by events. How children are nurtured, who does the nurturing, and how families can put children's thriving at their centre, are all matters rightly seen as urgent, but their potential competition with adult claims to fulfilment is less often acknowledged. The liberal position has genuine difficulties distinguishing between secular-led fashions of sexual behaviour and an authentically Christian sexual ethic. There is too small a space for ideas of mutual service and sacrifice for the sake of a communal good – whether that is a good of a particular household, of church, or of a wider vision of society. The 'progressive' vision is reluctant to admit that different individuals' rights may be in competition, even though (or perhaps because) a diversity of rights is central to its principles.

Meanwhile, the 'conservative' version seems over-neat, with impossibly tiny boxes for 'male' and 'female' social and sexual roles deliberately woven into a – distinctly strained – scriptural master narrative of 'God's plan'. The conservative solution to the social difficulties of competing individual rights is patriarchal authoritarianism, or 'male headship'. This attempts to re-establish pre-liberation male authority softened by female domestic influence. And the conservative view has virtues. It is rather a good thing to acknowledge that for communities to flourish there must be a mutual commitment to personal sacrifice for the greater good; and that a discourse that is *only* of competing individual rights will hurt people and impoverish society. And it is certainly true that societies look as if they will be easier to run when only a few of their members get executive power. When families were embodied and directed by fathers, they were a stable social and political unit in a way that the negotiated alliance of two individuals which makes up modern coupledom is not. But there was an enormous amount of buried misery in those male-headed units, and in the end that model also wastes lives, hurts people and impoverishes societies and households.

I do realize that it is not quite fair to dispatch a major debate in four paragraphs. But I suspect that my caricatures are recognizable. And although I've complained that the liberal and conservative narratives are 'untrue', 'untruth' of that kind isn't really the problem I have with them. Overarching narratives are always made by being ideologically selective. Each of these has clear claims as well as clear difficulties. My problem with them is that they have been in political opposition for so long that their opposition seems sometimes to be much of their point. And they don't seem to be thinking about faith itself, exactly, or even the character of Christian relationships, but what these groups think faith's markers ought to *look like* in relation to the big, powerful, secular world.

Here is a thought experiment. Suppose that the lives of those Christians committed enough to take any notice of our internal battles are being treated as a kind of necessary collateral damage for an ecclesial civil war that is essentially about something else? Suppose that the rift over sexuality, which in the Church of England has found its highest tension over same-sex relationships, is only a stalking horse for an underlying issue, which is the question of what the Church is called to stand for in wider public life?

Suppose that our division was itself handed to the Church on the back of a general cultural idolization of sex as transcendent liberation, and that the Church has ever since been reflexively breaking itself in pieces on a rock carved with the features of a secular idol?[10] One party saw one set of dangers and decided that the Church should mark its identity through a defiant purity code drawn from a mix of Scripture and myopic, male-dominated cultural nostalgia. (This was itself partly imported, like creationism, from the very different culture wars of the United States.) Perhaps in the process they also found themselves worshipping the purity-code version of sexuality as if it were all that God had to say to his children.

Meanwhile their opponents read the features of the idol as the next outworking of the kingdom's establishment on earth. They saw it as another move towards the greater kindness and civility to which they understood the world to be inevitably travelling in the long master-narrative of human progress, in which the good of any particular lobby group represented the good of all, no problems, no contradictions. A world-turned-upside-down revolution in which the marginal would sing Mary's song and yet in which, strangely, at the same time, the secular tellers of the story of improvement would continue quietly to decide who deserved to sing it next, and when. (The causes that deeply challenged the 'mighty in their seats', or that too obviously involved competing goods, would always be further down the list than the causes that they could more easily accommodate.) For this group, the blending of Christian and secular ethics would show only that history was doing what it should; what might happen to the Church's distinctiveness would be a decidedly secondary issue.

Behind these in turn lie very different visions of what the Church is, visions that are themselves – in the UK at any rate – tied up with the history of Reformation and of Establishment. Faced with a terrifying loss of social influence, indeed with

---

10 See Sam Brewitt-Taylor, *Christian Radicalism in the Church of England and the Invention of the British Sixties, 1957–1970* (Oxford: Oxford University Press), pp. 178–201.

the threat of effective disappearance as they haemorrhage congregations and are increasingly ignored in government,[11] the 'Puritan' and the 'Anglican' traditions within the Church of England (always uneasily and precariously held together) reach for solutions characteristic to their differing histories and identities.

The 'Puritans', with a vision of Christian community based on the set-apartness of 'holiness' code, and with separatism deeply driven into Calvinistic foundations, favour a sharp-edged division between a gathered holy people and the wilderness of the wickedly immoral world. Meanwhile, the 'Anglicans' read the whole world as God's field, in which sinners and saints mingle undetected, the Spirit blows where it wills, and only God can distinguish wheat from tares. This vision is, especially in England and Wales, underpinned by the ecclesiastical polity of establishment, which assumes that all in the nation belong by default to the assembly of the saved and leaves ultimate judgement to God.

The incompatibility of these ecclesiologies has been a problem for the Church of England more or less since that Church was invented in the sixteenth century. And in relation to sexual behaviour and relationships their usual solutions don't cope all that well with modern social realities. The quasi-separatist solution, dependent though it is on its selective harmonizations of New Testament behavioural advice, also relies both on the remaining social reach and resources of establishment and on secular retrospection. 'Holiness' looks like a mythically simpler world that resembles the 1950s more than it resembles biblical models. For quasi-separatists there is no place to go outside establishment except to become a gathered cult – but as the established Church becomes itself more and more gathered, the advantages of full separation sharpen.

---

11 The widespread hostility to the bishops' more cautious position on the Marriage (Same Sex Couples) Act of 2013 appears to have been a watershed moment for the episcopate in the House of Lords, the point where they appreciated, perhaps for the first time, what loss of influence really meant.

And the establishment default (you can't really call it a solution) takes no real account of the loss of Christendom, so that the generosity of its state ecclesiology tips into absurdity. When the cultural sense of belonging has disappeared from a significant percentage of your nation, how can you tell anyone anything at all about their behaviour and expect them to listen? Parish priests struggle with this problem every day, and not only in the area of sexuality. A generous elision of church and world (especially in a world that is forgetting church) means the disappearance of both the distinctiveness and the authority of any religious voice. There is nothing left to do but to go with the new normal for the culture with which you have merged.

And of course this is another cartoon of a complex situation. An awful lot has happened since the tense alliance of the Church's tribes split apart in the seventeenth century; there are a mass of subgroups not factored into this account; sex is not our only current problem. But when frightened tribes quarrel, they need something to quarrel about, a profound difference that diplomacy cannot mend. For the Church it is sexuality and how it is defined and understood: as sinful or liberating, dangerous or generous. Yet both sides agree that sexuality is central to what the Church stands for. And in doing that, we have chosen to remake ourselves around an image with which, ironically, the world outside the Church is already at least partly disenchanted.

If these irreconcilable differences continue to be the competing stories governing our dis-ease, then we have let the real Lord of all our doings, directing all our pathways and all our dissension, all our understanding of the Body of Christ and its institution in the big world, be the – already more than a little publicly tarnished – idol of sex itself. On our sexual behaviours, it seems, we stand or fall; we can do no other.

Which seems a pity.

3 MORES

The promises of Eros

Of course, it's easy to have a pop at the Church for being re-active to a wider cultural situation. Yet what else could she be? Such a huge change could not be ignored. In Bolz-Weber's thought-provoking book *Shameless,* she identifies sex, and its promise of a liberating transcendence, as the main competi-tion to religion for the hearts and minds of people, vulner-able in their needs and hopes, and longing for something to provide overarching meaning to their lives.[1] Although she is careful not to claim too much authority for the insight (she explicitly limits her field of research within the boundaries of her own worshipping community's personal experience), she is not alone in making it. In a recent radio programme, the Canadian anthropologist of sex Helen Fisher made a similar point, in striking form. In response to the suggestion that 'Love means everything', she replied, 'Now we expect Eros to make us gods.'[2] Not just worship, then, but deification.

What is it about Eros that is supposed to make us gods? What is so overwhelming about Love's 'meaning' that it should 'mean everything'? I think it is a reckless blend of two different and largely incompatible kinds of promise. One is for ecstasy. The other is for abiding romantic union. So this section leaves maps for dreams, for fantasies of what the erotic might seem to offer to life's meaning. It looks at poems, songs and stories rather than at statistics, to try to understand what it is people long for; and it has a go at looking at what, after all, they had to settle for.

'This live-long minute'

Ecstasy is an extreme experience, and its extremity is supposed to liberate our time-bound, creaturely senses from the crushing

---

1 Nadia Bolz-Weber, *Shameless* (Norwich: Canterbury Press, 2019).
2 Radio 4, *Analysis,* 2 June 2019.

weight of our creatureliness. It promises delight, lightness, freedom from cares. But it's not biddable, and it doesn't have staying power. Erotic delight makes no guarantee for the future,
and doesn't offer it much nourishment. Like its close coun-
terpart, religious ecstasy, it is elusive; like religious ecstasy, it
resists any system designed for its control. Its imitations can be
peddled, and are, relentlessly; but they deceive.

The ecstatic promise was very close, very seductive, in the
world in which I grew up. It wasn't alone. The romance of
transcendence beckoned from other competing or fashion-
ably allied powers: drugs, music and God. Ecstasy was hiding
behind the net curtains of the everyday, wearing different faces
but making the same offer: for an experience in which history
would be overmastered by the eternal moment, and you'd be
happy with the bargain.

Only, the thing is, there is no bargain. Ecstasy has no bar-
gains to make, no compunction for how creatures live in time.
It is evasive. Looking for it makes it even more so – and its costs
are very high. To live only for the ecstatic is to be cheated not
only of the ordinary everyday goodness of life but also, in the
end, even of the experience you seek. All that is left to do is to
look for a more extreme – often a more violent – version which
might still make you feel something sufficiently strongly. Of
course the 1970s counterculture loved de Sade; of course they
insisted on the 'beautiful prose' of the *Story of O*. They were
already bound into the law of diminishing returns. Nowadays
you don't have to witter on about 'beautiful prose' to get the
dubious thrills of extremity. Pornhub is always happy to oblige.

The logic of the ecstatic moment was summarized with a
bleak, witty, economical elegance by the libertine poet John
Wilmot, Earl of Rochester, who died in 1680, in his early thir-
ties, from a combination of syphilis and alcoholism. He wrote:

All my past life is mine no more,
The flying hours are gone,
Like transitory dreams giv'n o'er,
Whose images are kept in store
By memory alone.

The time that is to come is not;
How can it then be mine?
The present moment's all my lot;
And that, as fast as it is got,
Phyllis, is only thine.

Then talk not of inconstancy,
False hearts, and broken vows;
If I, by miracle, can be
This live-long minute true to thee,
'Tis all that Heav'n allows.[3]

This is a marvellous, despairing poem exerting all its skill to
say something untrue: that people live neither in the past nor
in the future. Rochester makes 'this live-long minute' into the
only real choice by relinquishing his hold on everything else: all
he has ever been, all he might be. His first move is to cancel the
'my' of 'my past life' and announce his history to be possessed
by time the robber, flying into unreachableness with the past
in its grip. The speaker is left with nothing: he wakes like one
mugged, with the rags of memory only the 'images' of 'transitory dreams'. As for the future, the speaker denies it any reality
at all, either as a form of imaginative potential or as a space for
the expression of faith: 'How can it then be mine?'

Rochester's poem therefore forbids hope, which relies on
imagining what might become. The living resonances of a personal history are also torn away, because he says memory is a
'store' of 'images' of what was once, and is no longer, real. The
sense of memory as an activity that lives in and changes the present is nowhere. Its elegant structure makes the verse close, claus-
trophobic: 'this live-long minute'. Though it promises to turn a
minute into a lifetime, it actually reduces a lifetime to a minute.

And it hints that even a minute is becoming too long a time to
retain, its integrity only intact by 'miracle'. The prison walls of
the poem press closer and closer together, threatening to crush

3 'Love and Life: A Song', in *The Penguin Book of Restoration Verse*, ed. Harold Love (London: Penguin, 1968), pp. 141–2.

our hero altogether, as in a Scooby-Doo cartoon, to the point where he loses his grip on even the smallest unit of time and can offer nothing to anybody at all. That point is coming, somewhere a little beyond the end of the poem's last line. The outcome of existentialism is advanced dementia. No one can really live like this. Hedonists who don't possess Rochester's grim wit just haven't paused to consider the logic of their position.

So is ecstasy a cheat? Not exactly. Rare glimpses of the joy beyond the rule of time matter very much indeed, and continue to do the work of meaning within both memory and longing. But ecstasy doesn't subsist on its own, and it can't be loved for its own sake. Worshipping sensation is not the same thing as meeting, or recognizing, or communicating, or loving, or caring. It doesn't, in the end, involve any other being than the self. Whether the sensation you worship is defined as sexual or as spiritual, if it begins and ends in self then it is bound to disappoint. Eternity *is* in love with the productions of time,[4] and we are made in order to practise our loves upon them, rather than to curve inward. When we 'love much', we learn how to meet God 'face to face'.[5] But we don't learn much about love by running after intense feelings.

'Journeys end in lovers meeting'?

So much for ecstasy. But what about romantic union? Is there something to worship there? The anthropologist Helen Fisher, when she suggested on the radio that Eros might make people into gods, wasn't talking about a life of brief, multiple encounters for their own sake. She was talking about those multiple encounters as necessary to the long modern search for 'the One'. The whole programme was about current routes to an ideal mate. Her diagnosis was that the sexual experimentations

---

4 William Blake, 'The Proverbs of Hell', in *The Marriage of Heaven and Hell* (written 1790–93). See https://poets.org/poem/proverbs-hell (accessed 09.01.2020).

5 Luke 7; 1 Corinthians 13.

of courtship have become massively extended. This is partly because the choice-potential has widened dizzyingly, indigestibly, via the increasingly popular option of online dating,[6] and partly because people's expectations of their permanent union (whether in marriage or in the more cautious form of cohabitation) have become extremely high. 'This is why the modern couple fails,' agreed the philosopher Pascal Bruckner, also interviewed on the programme. 'It is like an overloaded boat that sinks.' This ideal union is supposed to provide stability – *and* ecstasy; predictable support – *and* excitement; companionship – *and* challenge; longevity – *and* beauty. Yet the relationship between erotic delight and permanent union has always been tense and complicated, with Eros playing athwart the rules and conventions of vowed coupledom.

There is a long narrative tradition that takes the chaotic potential of 'lovers meeting' and allows it lots of play on condition that by the end it is firmly redefined as necessary public order. In the theatre, the 'comedy' genre, for which Shakespeare wrote, deploys marriage as a device for settling transgression. The disruptive powers of sexual ecstasy or other forms of rule-breaking around class, gender or sexuality are first expressed, then elaborated in all their wild glory, then quenched by a mass of weddings in the final scene. Even as the couples dutifully line up, the audience's response is partly shaped by the disruptions of the rest of the action.

Look at two well-loved Shakespeare plays, the first plays children are encouraged to see, viewed as light-hearted romps heading fast for a happy ending. *A Midsummer Night's Dream*, the background of which is a forced marriage (between Theseus and the captured Amazon Hippolyta) and a marital power-struggle (Oberon and Titania, usually played by the same actors), has a foreground so full of arbitrary magical reversals to people's desires that the final line-up feels arbitrary too. It is regulated at least as much by power as by desire.

---

6 A US data sample can be seen at https://flowingdata.com/2019/03/15/shifts-in-how-couples-meet-online-takes-the-top-spot/ (accessed 10.01.2020).

And his comedy *Twelfth Night* features a complex network of cross-dressing, gender ambiguity, social subversion and grief. First played before an audience of monarch and courtiers, the isolation and humiliation of a servant who dared to love his mistress and dream of power sours the orderly closure imposed by the final pairings-off.

The committed, long-term relationship is never a pure expression of personal delight. It is always tied to assertions of social order, always entangled in its mixture of power structures, common ideals and popular visions of what happiness might look like. It is impossible to talk about a theology of sexual ethics, or even about individual convictions on the subject, without taking dominant social expectations into account. If there are very strong underlying communal histories and traditions around gender, power and sexuality they will be powerful factors in determining the character of current relationships. Relationship choices do not only operate within private desires and feelings; nor are those feelings spontaneously generated. What happens in bed is only the inner world of something largely structured from the outside: a world that shapes what counts as desirable, tells you what to hope for; a world also of households, families, nurturing spaces for children, networks of wider kin and other relationships. Privacy is pressed into shape by the walls of this public world.

And this doesn't just apply to heterosexuality. Gay desire, and the politics around personal and gender identity, are influenced by definitions of 'normal': in our case those heterosexual, patriarchal, capitalist structures that sit so close to the surface of every relationship interaction, every piece of socialized self-understanding. All those personal choices and the shapes they choose and the identities they discover and the speed or slowness with which they dissolve and re-form – these things are structured by a complex interaction between the society that has been and the new agents of change it throws up. It's easier to see the new than to mark the old. When two men walk down the aisle hand in hand in their best clothes, carnations in their buttonholes, amid a cloud of confetti and a flurry of wedding presents, that's something old as much as it is something new. The way we live now is more influenced by the way we used to live than we are ready to acknowledge.

I talk so much about heterosexual patterns not just because it's what I know most about but precisely because of its cultural dominance, precisely because in doing so I am talking about well over 90 per cent of all adult relationships.[7] Books about Christian views of sexual desire nearly always talk about same-sex desire and about gender identity, because that's what attracts all the institutional anxiety. But secular, culturally embedded, heterosexual, ferociously gendered models of desire are talking really, really loud. They have been loud for a long time. These models have profound difficulties of their own. It is not plain to me that they are 'naturally' structured to express a distinctively Christian vision of the place of sexual desire in human relationships. So unless gendered heterosexual assumptions are looked at in their own right, and only then in relation to Christian holiness, I can't see how that vision of holiness can speak effectively to them at all. The two elide too insidiously for that. Agreed forms of social stability are not in themselves holy, and it's much too easy to treat them that way. (The marginal, the subversive, the disruptive, aren't automatically holy, either.) So I think it essential to look at the pictures of relationship our culture inherits, and what they tell us about the kinds of value projected onto sexual love.

The marriage plot

In a number of genres – the fairy tale, say, or the novel, or the novel's descendant the romcom – the structure generally known as the 'marriage plot' dominates. In it, marriage always represents a form of socialized closure which is intended to satisfy the reader's sense of order. The reader is supposed to gather that the

---

7 Office of National Statistics, 'Sexual orientation, UK: 2017' (2019), www.ons.gov.uk/peoplepopulationandcommunity/culturalidentity/sexuality/bulletins/sexualidentityuk/2017 (accessed 10.01.2020). The figure is 93.2 per cent.

protagonists have been satisfied too. Often marriage plots move towards moderately unlikely unions, where love overcomes some social barrier of wealth or class or the oppositions of authority figures. This is a genre manipulation. For even in 'marriage plot' terms, what marriage stands for is the stability of social relations, something for which Eros traditionally has little respect. Such plots attempt to fold the unstable into the orderly. Marriage plots are, therefore, about taming and regulating desire.

Nineteenth-century 'marriage plot' writers, like Charlotte Brontë or Anthony Trollope, often have to do a good deal of hard, far-fetched plotwork reconciling the pragmatics of social class, wealth, power and gender relations with the wishfully unlikely boundary-crossings of True Love.[8] Both of these authors were very aware of this unlikeliness. Brontë's most famous novel, *Jane Eyre*, has to rescue itself frantically from a tragic outcome, and features a mad wife who has to be killed off in a handy accident. Trollope's novels play with the tensions between marriage as financially based family alliance, made in order to keep or extend wealth and assets for an heir, and a more idealistic vision of it as companionate love match. Things work out strikingly seldom for his high-minded loyal heroines.[9] (The low-minded disloyal ones often do better.[10])

One disturbing novel of Trollope's, *He Knew He Was Right*, written before married women were allowed any separate legal identity from their husbands through the Married Women's Property Act, shows a fairly ordinary couple turning gradually under pressure into abusive husband and abused wife.[11] Trollope did not want to spell out the implication, but it is clear all the same – that the coercive structures of marriage itself at that time tended towards abuse.

---

8 Charlotte Brontë, *Jane Eyre* (1847); Anthony Trollope, a prolific English novelist of middle-class life writing between 1847 and 1882.

9 As in one of Trollope's best-loved novels, *The Small House at Allington* (1864).

10 See, for example, *The Eustace Diamonds* (1871), a novel with a successfully gold-digging heroine.

11 Married Women's Property Act (1882); Trollope, *He Knew He Was Right* (1869).

These are the stories we have been telling ourselves about
what love is and how it works. Our literature shows us things
that historical data or legal history cannot. *Jane Eyre* isn't just a
novel written by a shy, romantic, reclusive, myopic, ferociously
clever vicar's daughter in 1847. It isn't, even, just a novel that
(as Wikipedia puts it) 'revolutionised prose fiction'. Anyone
who reads it only to find out about 'prose fiction' is very much
missing the point. It's the novel that provides a template for the
cross-class Unlikely Romance, for a million million supermarket
paperbacks in which the craggy doctor falls for the humble
nurse. Complex and eloquent as it is, it's also a Cinderella
story, in which all the obstacles that ought to prevent a powerful man from recognizing a poor, proud, clever, not particularly
beautiful woman to be his soulmate are (finally) overcome. The
price exacted by its author for the unbelievableness of its plot is
the maiming of the powerful man. If Mr Rochester is blind, the
playing field is levelled. The romantic imitators of the formula
tend not to bother with that bit.

Brontë's powerfully influential fantasy was about a govern-
ess who married her employer in a love match of intellectual
equals. This was as cross-class as she dared to go – governesses
were often in the same social category as employers, genteel
women fallen on hard times. We can guess that the book, and
the mass of imitations it generated, fuelled the yearnings of
real nineteenth-century governesses, because the then-eminent
neurological doctor George Savage, writing in the 1880s in his
book *Insanity and Allied Neuroses*, complained that governesses were getting impossible ideas above their station and it
was sending them mad.

'To my mind,' he wrote,

> the governess's life is a very good example of the predis-
> posing causes of insanity . . . [She] is thrown into a purely
> subjective life, building castles in the air, dreaming what
> would be, or might be, if only intellect, the crown of man,
> had its proper sway, till at last the castles in the air become
> to her no longer fairy ideas, but actual realities. She thinks
> herself wedded to some wealthy nobleman; or, on the other

hand, she may develop ideas of suspicion, and fancy that every person about her is wishing to take from her her only possession, her virtue.[12]

Savage finds it difficult to believe that governesses might be sexually threatened, and absurd that poor women might dream of powerful men who took them seriously. But for the governesses themselves, the world looked different. Exploited and isolated, they knew they were in sexual danger. And they hoped they might find romantic union. People take fiction seriously when they need hope, and that was the form of hope available to them.

Marriage once represented, for women, the thing for which you were made: the status for which you desperately longed, because it conferred social dignity at the same time as it took away your separate identity and handed to your husband your rights, your safety and the most vulnerable and intimate parts of your body. So marriage was a prize, but its price was paid in bodily autonomy. You hoped for a soulmate, and dreamed about what that might mean, but reality was not set up to bear it out. The gamble was extraordinarily risky. And though change did follow the Married Women's Property Act, it was remarkably slow. Marital rape did not become a crime until 1993. In 2018, another quarter of a century later, a survey showed that 24 per cent of respondents still thought that rape was permissible in long-term relationships.[13]

Meanwhile, marriage for men meant a loss of bachelor freedoms, an acceptance of financial and family responsibility that brought youth to an end, and cramped any furtive sexual relationships, which might (as with Oscar Wilde) be with other men. In homosocial societies – and England was remarkably homosocial until well into the twentieth century – there were real obstacles to men and women being companions: they had not been taught

---

12 George Savage, 'Effect of Occupations', in *Insanity and Allied Neuroses* (1884), pp. 34–5.

13 End Violence Against Women/YouGov, *Attitudes to Sexual Consent* (2018), p. 3. See www.endviolenceagainstwomen.org.uk/wp-content/uploads/1-Attitudes-to-sexual-consent-Research-findings-FINAL.pdf (accessed 10.01.2020).

how to spend easy time together, or how to be friends. In such a world, the heterosexual couple, unless they were unusually emotionally skilful, were most likely to be forced into being a negotiated alliance of potentially opposing powers. Four centuries after Cranmer added 'the mutual society, help and comfort the one should have of the other' to his list of the goods of marriage in the Book of Common Prayer, the cultural and legal institution of marriage was still set up to reduce mutuality in the name of order.

In the first phase of twentieth-century 'sexual liberation', a mixture of influential voices expressed scepticism about how fit the institution of marriage was for any companionate purpose. Some of this came from feminist and some from queer sources (early members of Gay Liberation were later horrified at the equal marriage lobby; why yoke yourself to *that* toxic power-game?). Others, neither feminist nor queer, responded to the antinomian spirit of the age, rejecting marriage and feeling it more 'honest' only to promise for some version, shorter or longer, of the 'live-long minute'. And there was a tendency among both men and women, but perhaps particularly among men, to put off the burdens of responsibility and stay within the consequence-less pleasures of adolescence as long as possible.[14] The basic truth of attachment – that it is also constraint – was a massive hurdle for many with their eyes fixed on intense experience as the goal and meaning of life. The Who, in their breach of promise song 'Legal Matter' (1965), picked out an image of entrapped commitment straight out of childhood: a small boy with his head stuck in the 'garden rails' of respectable coupledom.[15]

The way we live now: some stats

Yet marriage, though in decline, has proved surprisingly resilient. While fewer people today get married, and cohabitation levels continue to climb, fewer of those who currently marry get

---

14 See www.natsal.ac.uk/natsals-12/results-archived-data.aspx (accessed 10.01.2020).

15 The Who, 'Legal Matter' (1965).

divorced than was the case in the 1960s–1980s. Fidelity continues to be prized.[16] The legal trappings of marriage are now better at safeguarding the rights of both parties than cohabitation – though not than civil partnership. Marriages also tend to last longer than cohabitations, and to offer more stability for children, for a variety of reasons which may include relative freedom from economic pressures, since the middle classes marry more readily than working-class couples do.

Weddings are very big business; dauntingly large sums are spent on them, and the conspicuousness of the consumption they attract sometimes appears to work as the most powerful of a couple's public statements of commitment, as one might expect in a society so bound into consumer values. Maybe the less well-off simply cannot afford to compete; every parish priest has presided at a first baby's baptism, for which no charge is made, repurposed as a kind of almost-wedding party. (Best clothes, a hog roast, the different families having a go at mutual harmony, a central ceremony around new life their social glue.) The institution of marriage, along with the flamboyant trappings of the wedding ceremony, has gained a curious, almost magical cachet: the long involved Amy Pond/River Song plotline of the Matt Smith series of *Dr Who* is a good example of how marriage could be regarded as simultaneously wonderful, sacred, binding – and yet temporary, fragile.

The National Survey of Sexual Attitudes and Lifestyles of 2003 (Natsal-2) documented a clear difference between women's and men's 'ideal relationship', with men much more likely to want non-monogamous permanent partnerships and somewhat less likely (especially in social classes IV and V) to want marriage or even cohabitation. Cohabitation was, however, on the rise as the 'ideal relationship' for both men and women.[17] By the time Natsal-3 was published, using data

---

16 See www.nhs.uk/news/lifestyle-and-exercise/results-of-uk-sex-survey-published/ (accessed 10.01.2020), which summarizes the *National Survey of Sexual Attitudes and Lifestyles* (Natsal-3) of 2012 and reports a growing disapproval of partners who 'cheat'.

17 See www.natsal.ac.uk/natsals-12/results-archived-data.aspx (accessed 10.01.2020).

from 2010–12, the trend towards cohabitation had strength-ened further.[18] The national statistics on marriage for 2017 show that about half the UK population is married, with same-sex marriages constituting about 2 per cent of marriages overall. When cohabitation figures are added, the proportion of the population in couple relationships climbs to 61.4 per cent.[19] Those who marry tend to have children with higher life-chances – but then there is a strong correlation between higher education and income levels, planned parenthood at a later age, and opting for marriage.[20]

Natsal-3 also supports the view that high expectations of relationships contribute to their failure for modern couples. A paper on relationship breakdown extrapolated from its data concluded that the reasons given for breakdown were roughly the same for married as for cohabiting couples, and that primary reasons given were 'grew apart' and 'arguments'. Adultery/unfaithfulness came second, lack of respect/apprecia-tion third. However, in the UK four times as many women as men (15.9 per cent as against 3.7 per cent) cited domestic vio-lence as a reason for relationship breakdown, and the authors of the study add that the real figure is likely to be much higher than this – already one in six relationships – since domestic violence goes under-reported. Marriages tended to last longer than cohabitations, though they broke up on the same grounds. The authors concluded that

the predominance of reasons reported, such as grew apart, arguments and lack of respect/appreciation, suggests a dete-rioration in the quality of relationships and echoes research

18 See www.thelancet.com/action/showPdf?pii=S0140-6736%2813 %2962035-8 (accessed 10.01.2020).

19 See www.ons.gov.uk/peoplepopulationandcommunity/population andmigration/populationestimates/bulletins/populationestimatesby maritalstatusandlivingarrangements/2002to2017 (accessed 10.01.2020).

20 Crawford, Goodman and Greaves, 'Cohabitation, Marriage, Relationship Stability and Child Outcomes: Final Report', *IFS Report R87*, Institute for Fiscal Studies, 2013, pp. 17–18. See www.ifs.org.uk/comms/comm120.pdf (accessed 10.01.2020).

over recent decades reflecting the high expectations of self-fulfilment in contemporary marriage and cohabitation and the increasing unacceptability of emotionally and personally unsatisfying partnerships.[21]

They recommend that, in the wake of the high social cost to adults and children from relationship breakdown in mental health and other kinds of well-being, their results be deployed to support relationship counselling. They also express serious disquiet about the UK's domestic violence problem, which is much worse than for the equivalent study made in France, recommending urgent intervention.

Eros in the marketplace

Sex doesn't seem to be a very satisfactory god, in terms of either fleeting pleasure or long-term contentment. And in fact sex, like drugs and rock'n'roll, the other outdated deities of transcendent promise, is bound more firmly than ever into the dominant world of the marketed consumer commodity. Sex is part of the 'norms of capitalist free exchange', remarks the cultural critic Amia Srinivasan: these norms regulate both short- and long-term relationships, control the agreed transfer between buyer and seller, mean that you can cancel if the product doesn't give satisfaction.[22] Neither the reckless gift of the moment nor the True Love vision has enough structural staying power to manage on its own without the exchange model to regulate it.

For long-term relationships there is a complex interplay between the dreams of felicity prompted and nourished by a million happy-ending stories and the reality of how a relationship might feel under the pressures of 'real life'. 'Happy ending'

21 https://journals.plos.org/plosone/article?id=10.1371/journal.pone.0174129 (accessed 10.01.2020).

22 Amia Srinivasan, 'Does Anyone Have the Right to Sex?', *London Review of Books* 40:6, 22 March 2018.

is an odd way to describe a commitment that could take 60 years to play out; it is extremely vulnerable to cost-benefit analysis at any point along the way.

Transactional relationships are anything but new, of course. Trollope's middle-upper-class brides were being displayed as financial assets and were themselves on the hunt for a 'good match'. Longer ago yet, Shakespeare's sardonic eye pointed out the parallels between dowry systems and short-term bought sex in the discomfiting plot and sour jokes of his play *Measure for Measure* at the turn of the sixteenth century.[23] Such arrangements differed from the present, however, in that men were always buyers of women and that the financial nature of the bargain was explicit. The marketplace principle now works all ways round without necessarily being honest about its transactional nature. Different serial monogamies for different stages of life are normal; for the ageing rich, youth can be purchased by proxy, in the shape of a younger partner. Our Prime Minister[24] is not sure how many children he has; this has not prompted his elderly Conservative electors to wonder whether he might have an irresponsibility problem. The President of the United States regularly changes his wife for a younger model.

A programme like *Love Island* makes transaction showily explicit, but its mechanisms work, in a more private but fleeting format, for the increasingly popular option of online dating. You advertise to get attention, using a formula that imagines what might command it. You showcase physical attractiveness, of course, conforming as far as possible to the agreed stereotypes of the culture, but you also curate an arrestingly unique, but not *too* quirky, personal detail which can be indicated in a brief glance. You lie a bit, but not too much, in case you meet up and are rumbled. The online formula provides 'choice' on a scale that cannot be matched within physically

23 The recent RSC production (summer 2019), directed by Greg Doran, deliberately brings out the #MeToo element in its plot line.

24 As of September 2019 (and referring to the election of Conservative leader, not the General Election of December 2019).

118

confined social encounter, and this allows for the algorithmic honing of preference.

There are disadvantages to these advantages. It's true that you're not just stuck with whatever happens to be locally available, but choice also makes it harder to settle for any particular option or to decide that a search is really over. Working within preference settings reduces risk but may harden prejudice (including in some disturbing ways, for example in solidifying racist mindsets, or reinforcing the extent to which men of all ages seem to want to sleep with teenagers), and makes the unexpected much less likely, both good and bad.[25] That said, online dating can also make formal space for more vulnerable voices swamped or silenced in the hierarchies of ordinary life, most obviously for LGBT+ users.

There is a good deal of controversy about the effect of online mechanisms on relationships. What is clear, though, is that online dating is pragmatic. It is an efficient use of time. It uses a consumerist model to benefit the user, and it presents options for that user to select between – though the user is, at the same time, being selected too. It applies the mechanisms of shopping to love; seeker and sought become products. The fantasy of sex as gift sits very ill with online selection processes. It is more like getting the perfect cup of coffee, or the perfect meal; its 'falling in love' is rather a lot more like 'falling in love' with exactly the right house in exactly the right location on a Zoopla list. It gives the seeker a sense of control; but then it also burdens the seeker with – a sense of control.

However, in modern environments where physical social encounters are fewer, communities more virtual and less local, workplaces increasingly hazardous locations for romance, working hours long, and much of the rest of life happening online, it makes sense. Just not transcendent sense.

Sex, for the world outside the Church, is not straightforwardly the means to fulfilment. It is seen as a necessary good, like food; but not an automatic road to joy. It is strongly bound

25 See www.nytimes.com/2011/11/13/fashion/online-dating-as-scien tific-research.html (accessed 10.01.2020).

DESIRE

into consumer practices; it is used to sell almost everything else; it regulates itself in forms very like the regulation of other consumer goods. Yet at the same time human relationships are being required to bear the spiritual weight once carried by religion, which puts even more pressure on an already difficult area.

Long-term relationships are assumed to have a sexual basis that ought to be lively, satisfying and frequent, though sex turns out to happen far less frequently than we are told it ought to, particularly in the UK culture of long and unpredictable working hours.[26] The gap between actual experience and the powerful myth of satisfaction creates disappointment. Short-term encounters are often explicitly and sometimes mutually commodified. Shortfalls in fulfilment are perceived as good reasons for ending relationships, including relationships that are central to a cross-generational network of kin and community, because fulfilment is defined as an individual rather than a collective good. Marriage is a little less of a casualty in this regard than other domestic arrangements for relationship, but then those who marry self-select for long-term commitment and often have less pressure of other kinds upon them.

Women continue to be the main carers for children, but are more frequently doing it by themselves, or combining the care for the children of several couple-histories joined contingently through the latest relationship. More and more people live alone. Families lose sight of their members, find it difficult to work out where their borders are, find that people drop in and out of those wider networks as relationships fail. It can sometimes seem that love flourishes in spite of, rather than because of, the cultural over-valuation of sexual pleasure.

26 *Sexual Attitudes and Lifestyles in Britain: Highlights from Natsal-3*, www.natsal.ac.uk/media/2102/natsal-infographic.pdf (accessed 10.01.2020).

4 MARRIAGE

'As the angels in heaven'

Theologians pondering Christian understandings of sexuality usually spend a lot of time talking about marriage. They do this while pointing out that marriage embodies the Christian vision for sexual union, which, yes, it does. And the way they talk about it tends to use marriage as a sacred metaphor for the divine–human encounter.

The prefaces to both *Common Worship* and the Book of Common Prayer marriage services declare that the joining of a couple foreshadows the eschatological meeting between Christ and his Church.[1] They identify marriage, too, as a sign of the abundance that pours out from God to his children, as in the miracle of the wedding at Cana, where Jesus transforms water in great quantity to become not just wine but *really good* wine.[2] They observe, sometimes somewhat indirectly, that it is the smallest possible model (two people) of the unified and loving community participating in the adoration of the divine Creator, God in relationship. And they say that marriage is a 'gift of God in creation', a divine good inscribed in fleshly intimacy, close to the absolute basics of who human beings are and how they might flourish. It is a place for making new life, a kind of echo to the world-making power in which God delights.

These different scripturally derived concepts allow theologians to spend time on laying out the patterned, interlocking logic of the marriage sign, systematizing it all into a vision of creative divine perfection, with earthly marriage laid out as its working model. And it all makes sense.

But the sense it makes points beyond the nature of human marriage. Its sense lies in the way that vowed human joining

---

1 Revelation 21.1–7; Matthew 25.1–13; 'Marriage' and 'Solemnization of Matrimony', in *Common Worship: Pastoral Services*, 2nd edn (London: Archbishops' Council, 2011).

2 John 2.1–12.

allows us to see, and even to know, something of the limitless intimacy of God with his beloved creatures, something
of the creative potential of God's mingling with the limits of
our fleshly stuff. The qualities of marriage are illustrative of
this further vision. These metaphors point beyond their illustrations to something else; the illustrations themselves are still
firmly earthbound.

God's love will not be confined inside the marriage metaphor. Nor will the metaphor, pointing as it does towards the
perfection of divine relationships, accommodate all the other
things that marriage is – in time and space and history with
flawed people shaped by less-than-perfect societies. Marriage
is something *people* do. They do it within cultures that have
particular shapes, constraints and structural oppressions. And
in this chapter it has seemed important to me to start from
there, from the things people do and are calling love and marriage, which are a long, long way from the visions of divine
perfection the *idea* of marriage might illustrate. God may bless
marriage, seeing, in its desperately fragile, crazily hopeful mixture of shared faith and intimacy, a deep longing for the eternal
recognition all his creatures yearn towards. God may honour
its potential for nourishing new life. But the project of joining
God's love with the goods of marriage is not airtight, not a
double-locked argument in which everything matches everything else. There are echoes, similitudes. And, then, there are
differences.

When I tell a couple, in the course of discussing the 'preface'
they will hear read at their church wedding, that their joining
is like the joining of Christ and his Church, they tend to look,
at best, blankly polite. This is because even the most devout of
them are there to think about their wedding. They are just not
focused on the eschatological union of the universal Church.
Thinking about marriage, as St Paul pointed out, is about as
different from thinking about the end-times as anything could
possibly be.[3]

---

3 1 Corinthians 7.25–39.

This is why I find the theological move that reads back from the metaphorical nature of marriage to prescriptions about what marriage should be a kind of category mistake. It has all the beguiling deception of a closed loop, and I do realize that systematic thinking operates like that. But metaphors work, and work powerfully – there's nothing weak or unreal about metaphor – because they are *not* closed. Were all bread consecrated, all water holy and all sexual union sacred, creation would need neither blessing nor redemption. But unblessed bread nourishes and ordinary water washes away literal dirt. Bread, water and sex are already good things, but they point beyond themselves to something they, in themselves, cannot be. Of resurrected bodies Jesus said, 'They neither marry nor are given in marriage, but are like angels in heaven.'[4] Taking and being taken are not, then, inscribed into our eternal relationships, which is something of a relief, I think. In the world of perpetual light we might at last know the one equal possession that eludes us upon earth. But that is in a place beyond the fears and hopes of time.

One flesh

It isn't necessary to read descriptive visions of ideal sexual union prescriptively. When, in Genesis 2.24, the narrator looks at the primordial couple, a couple who are not 'married' because there is as yet no society to stamp their union with that form, and says, 'for this reason a man leaves his father and mother and clings to his wife, and they become one flesh', it's not a defensive recipe for heterosexual social order. It's a description of what happens in life. The genders are put there in the sentence because that's the shape that families take in a world where sex results in babies, and communities are built round the biological inevitability of that. So the words aren't written to remind people only to have the kind of heterosexual sex that results in babies; that's not deemed necessary. They are written to show how the encounter

4 See Mark 12; Matthew 22; Luke 20.35–36.

involved in sex is more like looking in a mirror than meeting a stranger; of how our place in the human communities to which we belong will shift as we grow up from being someone's child to being someone's spouse; of how mutual recognition of self in another will make a new home for the future. These are goods for which human beings might reasonably hope.

That these good things happen and go on happening across the long, bitter divide between men and women is an ordinary, God-given miracle, the everyday redemption of a history of oppressive structures that impels male–female interaction to be fearful, often violent, frequently mutually uncomprehending. And yet so many people manage to love across the divide.

It might even be a little *easier* to imagine harmony in homosexual partnership, given the gender bias in how the power structures of the world operate – though data emerging from countries who legalized same-sex unions longer ago than the UK doesn't indicate that same-sex couples are finding long-term commitment any easier than heterosexuals.[5] All the same, it is worth pondering. The 'same' in 'same-sex' could make mutual recognition easier and more likely, rather than the fearful identification of difference. (That was certainly the implication of Augustine's observation that had marriage been intended for companionship God would have given Adam a male partner.[6]) There might be some freedoms from the stereotypes of particular gendered roles, a freer and more creative play in the joint discernment of shared responsibility. Domestic stability is deeply desirable, very steadying in an uncertain world: perhaps it took the same-sex marriage act to help us notice how desirable it is. It is remarkable that the public and social responsibility of

---

5 See 'Same-Sex Divorces', *The Economist* (11 January 2020), p. 25, which quotes a leading divorce lawyer as saying that in same-sex divorces 'all the same things crop up [as in heterosexual divorce]'. Data from the Netherlands, where same-sex marriage has been legal for 15 years, shows marriages between women breaking up at a much higher rate (30 per cent) than marriages between men (15 per cent) or than heterosexual marriages (18 per cent).

6 See Robert Song, *Covenant and Calling: Towards a Theology of Same-Sex Relationships* (London: SCM Press, 2014), p. 48.

the institution of marriage is even wanted, a kind of massive civic compliment to a culture which, historically, hasn't been exactly welcoming of same-sex relationships until very recently. (David Cameron, the Prime Minister presiding over the passing of the Marriage (Same Sex Couples) Act in 2013, was still voting against repealing Section 28 in the year 2000.) There seems to be something about marriage, specifically marriage, that is understood and embraced as more, and greater, than a contractual partnership. Did it take the longing for marriage from an excluded group for us to notice how valuable it was? I don't think we are in a position, either as a society or as a Church, to disdain a yearning for blessed, committed, long-term fidelity.

In spite of everything, people both homosexual and heterosexual do somehow manage decent amounts of companionate, vowed lives of nurture, expressed in literal births, new generations, creative partnerships. When the words of Genesis 2.24 express love as 'clinging' to a spouse at this point in the story of the Fall, just as Eve has been created, they seize upon a moment of mutual felicity and send it forwards through the Fall into history and culture. This generational realignment, this clinging, will indeed keep on happening through time, in the histories made by families. Adam and Eve's union makes the story of the Fall a narrative of hope as well as of sin, mistake and destruction. Jesus refers back to the words of Genesis 2.24 sorrowfully in a discussion of the hard-heartedness of divorce, not because he feels a sudden need to point out that men should only desire women, but because he is so struck that love should fail, that men should be so 'hard-hearted'.

For the recognition that redeems us from violence does not *need* to be between men and women, and regeneration is not always expressed in literal procreation. The world will continue to be peopled, even while the kinds of love some turn towards will not result in making babies. Come to that, there are a great many isolated and neglected children in the world already, for whom love is deeply needed. The anxiety expressed about procreation being necessary to the marriage bond only makes sense if you assume that most people, were they allowed to, would really long for homosexual partnership, or that most heterosexual partnerships would prefer to be childless. Neither of these fears is borne out by evidence. Is all creation literal? Are we not following the divine pattern of making when we make things other than babies?

Nowadays we concede that the female half of humanity does not *have* to spend the whole of her prime in child-bearing and child-rearing. We need also to concede the logic of that situation. Contraception allows for other kinds of creation to happen as they could not before. As any mother will be able to affirm, the work of baby-making and subsequent child-rearing brings almost everything else to a halt – art, music, buildings, poetry, sculpture, all kinds of machines or ideas – anything that involves concentrating for more than 30 seconds together. When we imagine the gender gaps, prejudices and miscommunications of the past, we need at the same time to imagine the enormous stresses upon all sexually active women of being constantly pregnant or nursing, and the effect this had upon their *actual* ability (let alone other people's perceptions of their ability) to do anything else at all. No regrets for the loss of that world. The divinely creative work of humankind is very various, and enough people will want to make babies in their own right time. 'Natural' is not the same as 'good'. Good is found in the way we encounter God and each other in relationship, the image of God in our readiness to build and to reconcile rather than to break.

And while it is true that relationships fail, the project of fidelity, supporting a whole network of kin and community relationships, seems the right place for the holding and nurturing of desire. Not as a consumer experiment, but as a vocational calling named marriage, turned outward as well as inward to be one of a range of ways in which human life acknowledges its mutual dependence and connectedness.

'Fully known'

The most popular biblical reading for a wedding is 1 Corinthians 13. Those who choose it do so for a variety of reasons, but big among them is the sense that 'to know fully, even as I am fully known' expresses a profound need of the soul. Along the way, Paul talks about the negotiations necessary to trustful relationships:

> Love is patient; love is kind; love is not envious or boastful or arrogant or rude. It does not insist on its own way; it is not irritable or resentful; it does not rejoice in wrongdoing, but rejoices in the truth. It bears all things, believes all things, hopes all things, endures all things.

Paul is not talking about eros. He is describing another kind of love, distinguished in Greek culture from the wilder, less biddable characteristics of sexual desire. But wedding couples nevertheless see in his description something they deeply want. This love is unconditional, absolutely committed, attentive, reciprocal, even sacrificial, hallowing and carrying the past (it 'bears all things'), trusting the present (it 'believes all things') and projecting its joy towards the future (it 'hopes all things').

If I were to draw a parallel between the project of human sexual love and the love of God I would start with the love of God and run the metaphor that way round. 'God loves everyone', we say to small children, and that is true. But God's love for 'everyone' isn't general in the way that that phrase implies. God's love is the only love that can be both exclusive and universal, and that's not available to human beings because they are finite. For each soul loved, the divine love is intense and particular, infusing each lived moment with a fierce and steady attention. It is closely parallel to the attention of a lover to the beloved, though the abiding presence of mother to infant or the tender attention of a father to the vulnerability of a small child is there as well. When a mother contemplates an infant, a father his toddler, a lover the face of the beloved, time retreats a little to make room for an exclusive, self-forgetful concentration upon the being and nature of another person.[7] We are

---

7 Isaiah 49.15; Hosea 11.3; Isaiah 61.10.

granted just a little glimpse of the eternal when we risk the tenderness of loving a person in time.

The exclusive two-person unit of marriage makes space for a love-project that emulates the steady and complete attention of God. Of course that is crazy; of course it fails more often than it succeeds; of course that kind of mutual knowledge is essentially, and perhaps mercifully, out of reach. It is difficult to pay each other steady attention, but that does not mean we should not try. It is, after all, a 'gift of God in creation' – like redemption, wrested by grace, indeed by miracle, from an impossible set of demands in an impossible context. It is a discipline of love in and of itself. Not the only one, and not in itself the foundation of the universe. But one of the means by which we learn the nature of the sacrificial, the generous, by which we pursue the lifelong vocation to learn another person as well as we possibly can, good and bad, through all the extraordinary changes wrought by time and change and ageing and sickness, along with the betrayals of sin, all the way to the final change of death, to and beyond and through the constant experience of loss.

God knows, through Christ, what it is to do that work: to live and love and give of the self, pouring out your little store of time until greed and inattention and the violent structures of the world break the person you are on its crosspiece – yet where that defeat, inevitable though it is, is absolutely not the last word. Marriage is one of the ways we might have a glimpse of the cost involved in the project of time-bound loving, but also of the vastness of its blessing. In it we could learn both to know and to bear to be known, so that at the last we might be assisted to endure and embrace the weight of God's particular and personal knowledge with hope, and faith, and love.

5

Self-Fashioning

Identity and personhood

This is a chapter about identity. At the moment understandings of personal identity are fast-changing; by the time this book is out it will already have dated. And the many current debates about identity, including but not solely those that centre on gender, are bound into heated arguments about sexuality and culture, as well as into wider arguments about the nature of selfhood.

In Christian thought, human personhood transcends sex and exists inviolate, independent of all other cultural constructions to which human beings are subject, including (but not limited to) those of gender.[1] At the same time, these Christian understandings acknowledge that the human person is so deeply entangled with human community in its being and doing that the individual cannot be talked about in separation from community, for good or ill.[2]

So whatever human personhood is, looked at through the Christian frame, it is not an untrammelled, separate, limitless selfhood, claiming the satisfaction of all its desires as soon as they arrive. It is shaped by the constraints of love and connection as they are expressed in the two great commandments.[3] It recognizes and honours the limits of the fragile human body. It expects an eternity in which it will be fully defined by love. The kingdom of love for which Christians wait and work makes

---

1 Mark 12.25; Matthew 22.30; Luke 20.35, 36; Galatians 3.28.
2 For example, 1 Corinthians 12.12–27.
3 Matthew 22.35–40; Mark 12.28–34; Luke 10.27.

the demands of collective nurture upon them, including upon who they think they are. Those demands, as Jesus pointed out a number of times, are high.[4]

Modern selfhood

This chapter looks at selfhood – and particularly at a contradiction in the idea of the modern self. On the one hand, we seem to believe that we have the power to make ourselves in the image we want to over time. On the other, we see ourselves as much more helpless than that, much more driven and shaped by other forces. I've taken the word 'self-fashioning' as a place to start thinking about this, because just at the moment the selves we perform for others have a lot of weight given to them. There are plenty of promises around that people can make themselves into whatever they choose to be.

So I'm going to look at the history of how we got our modern ideas of self. At what that means for how modern human beings intervene (as they continually do and must) in the stories of themselves. At how an individual's story fits with – and makes demands upon – the collective stories of communal identity. At the dominant cultural models shaping our self-fashioning decisions. At the limits of what can be willed for bodies and minds. At the nature of self-love – and self-disgust, and self-hatred – in a society that is inclined to make the self the focus of desire.

Of course I don't have answers. But I have tried to think about identity in ways that are not confined to the highly contested gender boundaries upon which so much current anxiety is focused. Sex and gender are large parts of our modern self-understanding, and for that reason this chapter must talk about them, but the unanswerable question I am asking is larger than that. How do people know *who they are*?

---

4 Mark 8.36; Matthew 16.26; Luke 14.28–30; Matthew 16.24–26; Luke 9.23; Matthew 5.29.

The beginnings of modern identity

Self-fashioning is a term coined by the literary historian Stephen Greenblatt.[5] He used it to describe the way people of the sixteenth century constructed their identities round the practice of performing, or 'fashioning', social roles. Clothes, body language, speech, action – all contributed to the self that was shaped and presented to the world.

Greenblatt chose the verb 'fashion' deliberately. Its use was relatively new in the sixteenth century, and its meaning hovered significantly between indicating a pure creative act and denoting a form of deliberate, human-led, social shaping. So Miles Coverdale, translating Psalm 139 in the 1530s, has the psalmist say to God, 'thou hast fashioned me behind and before'; but when Edmund Spenser announces in 1590 that he intends his poem *The Faerie Queene* to 'fashion a gentleman', the verb, though still about making, gets several notches closer to our modern noun 'fashion', a word not about plain essentials but about ambiguous coverings – disguises that yet reveal, or revelations that yet disguise.

Greenblatt wasn't making a point about masks, with a 'real' self underneath. On the contrary, he was saying that performing identity constructed what the 'real' even was. He thought that the sixteenth century gave a clue to how modern people understand themselves; and that their world, sometimes called the 'early modern' world, shaped the society we know today.

Although he showed identities shaped by cultural pressures, he was really interested in the spaces people made for their own choices – the 'dance' of self-making which an individual could participate in, within narrow restrictions. You couldn't choose not to be a king, if that's what you were born to be, but you could choose what kind of king you fashioned yourself into. He called this 'an increased self-consciousness about the fashioning of human identity as a manipulable, artful process'.[6]

---

5 Stephen Greenblatt, *Renaissance Self-Fashioning* (Chicago: University of Chicago Press, 1980).

6 Greenblatt, 'Introduction', *Renaissance Self-Fashioning*, p. 2.

Reading Greenblatt is quite an odd experience. Sometimes he seems to be saying that people have no choices at all about who they are. At other times he focuses particularly on the separate, private intelligence making its performance choices, something called a 'self'. He finishes his book on a personal note; its final sentence acknowledges, in a gallant flourish of self-defeat, his own 'overwhelming need to sustain the illusion that I am the principal maker of my own identity'.[7]

Greenblatt's idea excited a lot of people. (Admittedly most of them were academics in the disciplines of history, literature and cultural studies, but they were quite excited, all the same.) He seemed to be describing something they recognized, something people were still doing. The personal paradox with which Greenblatt ended his book, speaking out for self-making at the same time as declaring the process illusory, seemed to articulate a living, urgent, fundamental unease for modern understandings of self and identity.

Need and choice

Over the 40 years since Greenblatt's book came out that unease has sharpened. As assertions of personal identity acquire increasingly visible political meanings, and as the pluralism of modern living conditions offers a much more dispersed and diverse range of social meanings for individuals to inhabit, the questions he asked have become more urgent. Is identity about where you belong in society – something you don't completely choose – or is it something you can make yourself, individually? The term 'identity' is used very flexibly by people, located at any point on a frictionless slide between an externally imposed social definition and an internally chosen, self-fashioned being. Few usages are entirely one or entirely the other, but the balance of the mix varies widely. This matters because, depending on that balance, different kinds of cultural authority may be claimed for personal identity.

7 Greenblatt, *Renaissance Self-Fashioning*, p. 257.

An identity claim based on 'choice' is an option, so it's more difficult to claim it as a 'need'. There's some social pushback on it. To take a real example: there might be plenty of tolerant space for a semi-ironic youth subculture which plays about with ideas of mortality – skulls and so on – but the young paramedic with 'DEATH' tattooed on his forearm has got a problem. He's told by his supervisor that a very ill person seeing his tattoo will be terrified by it, and so it must go. The paramedic solves his problem by going on shift with a plaster covering the tattoo. DEATH hidden by a dressing is, it's true, an unfortunate way of signifying the paramedic's vocation – but that way he keeps his job. Then, in his time off, he can remove the plaster and inscribe 'DEATH' in a context where its meaning is nicely bounded to mean – well . . . not what it says.

An identity claim that rests on need is on much stronger ground than a choice claim. Need may invoke a particular, practical set of circumstances, or an essentialist premise of some kind, or a person may simply cite authoritatively strong feeling and not speculate about causation. Yet it still has another stage to get through. Needs, asserted on their own, run the risk of making you look like a victim, humiliated rather than proud. So often people join up need with personal agency by reaching for the language of rights; they redefine necessity as a necessary liberty. This has happened deliberately in the world of disability discourse, where the move from need to right has evident moral force, but it is not confined there. So, for example, there is a world of difference between defining a desire for an identity as originating in a distanced pathology called 'gender dysphoria' – which privileges need but minimizes agency – and naming the desired new 'trans' self as a positively embraced identity powerful enough to rename traditional gender as 'cis'.

Identities of want

The freedoms of individual choice are widely accepted to be the birthright of everyone in Western modernity. They are seen as an appropriate moral claim people should make upon the society into which they have been born. The boundaries of such a claim are the familiar boundaries of 'do no harm', grounded in equally widely accepted principles of mutual tolerance.

Some claims clearly go beyond those boundaries. Take for example the 'incel' claim (the word is constructed from 'involuntary celibate'). Themselves overwhelmingly male, they claim that having sex is a 'right' they are being denied. The point at which Reddit at least in part shut down their online conversations was when it became too openly clear that such a 'right' included the right to rape, and thus to limit the personal freedoms of another.[8]

The issue here is really straightforward, in a way. It's a completely unacceptable claim. But what happens to people whose identity is grounded on what they cannot have and must not do? It can't be a choice; so is it a need? But to be defined by your impossible need is unendurable; so the 'incel' makes the next obvious move towards claiming personal liberty. It's not *just* a need, he says. It's a right. He is being denied a right to sex. The identity he holds is so enfolded in deep contradiction that he might quite sincerely claim to be suffering a form of torment.

Incels argue that 80 per cent of women will have sex with only 20 per cent of men – figures that sound a little exaggerated, but perhaps such men only bother to count conventionally desirable women. They point out that most of the lucky ones are likely to be white, middle class, well educated, rich, good looking. Why, they say, should the poor, the ugly, the non-white guy be denied the one thing he really, really needs? Do the pressures of a racist society which rewards riches, beauty and whiteness with sexual access really not provide a sufficient reason for an underdog to object to his sexual starvation? What would be the limits of such an objection, given a 'right' to sex? Would rape look more like shoplifting for food to a starving man?[9]

8 See https://en.wikipedia.org/wiki/Incel (accessed 10.01.2020).

9 This issue is discussed in Amia Srinivasan, 'Does Anyone Have the Right to Sex?', *London Review of Books* 40:6, 22 March 2018.

Which makes it extremely clear why any analogy between sex and food is dangerously misleading.[10] It only works if potential partners become consumable; and eating people really *is* wrong. For the incel, a beautiful woman is not a person but an impossibly priced good, provocatively displayed behind a glass window. Yet which human group can claim to be the group of 'real' persons requiring nourishment from lesser beings? Men? Women? The rich? The beautiful? The strong? Or none of the above? What happens when a claim is made that nevertheless trespasses upon the territory of another's identity? Once desire is reframed as a right, what should be done with the impulse to violence against another that is almost bound to accompany it?

All around the incel as he lives his life, the dominant consumerist world will parade before him an endless procession of apparently sexually available women to represent the priced goods of desire – cars, underwear, shoes, holidays, chocolate, jewellery, and of course sex itself. A man without power is constantly being told that his human worth is measured by objects he cannot afford. None of this is an excuse for rape – but humiliation dreams of redress. Sometimes he is encouraged to think this way – as in the notorious 2007 Dolce & Gabbana adverts, which appear to be showing stylized preliminaries to a gang rape.[11] The world of mainstream porn, and the online threats of trolls, head towards rape fantasies with a striking swiftness and frequency. The only way to dream of freedom, when you are defined by lack, is to imagine – and sometimes to plan – revenge. The briefest of looks at the internet, that ultimate libertarian space, suggests that a very large number of unhappy men are doing exactly that.

---

10 Correspondence between Rebecca Solnit and Amia Srinivasan in *London Review of Books* on this subject, 2018. See www.lrb.co.uk/the-paper/v40/no6/amia-srinivasan/does-anyone-have-the-right-to-sex #letters (accessed 09.01.2020).

11 See https://metro.co.uk/2015/03/18/dolce-gabbana-in-hot-water-again-after-gang-rape-ad-campaign-resurfaces-just-days-after-ivf-furore-5108624/ (accessed 10.01.2020).

Assent, refusal and subversion

Self-shaping assertions happen in the world. Even though they are sometimes articulated – and critiqued – as if without reference to anything but themselves, they actually need endorsement. A performed self, however 'real', relies on the perceived authority of its performance, an authority that is granted by those who watch rather than by the performer. That is the vulnerability of the claimed identity, the huge vulnerability for the person reliant for cultural acceptance on responses to (for example) social media posts, or personal pronoun choice.

And all self-shaping assertions are themselves cultural assertions, so that their demands for acceptance may impose genuine cultural disruptions and changes – perhaps deliberately, perhaps involuntarily. A self-shaping demand that insists on wider cultural adjustment will not necessarily increase social tolerance: the effect may be quite the reverse. The person making the demand may genuinely find their identity compromised by refusal; yet the person withholding acceptance may have their own identity vested in a cultural norm that is breaking down or altering under the pressure of that same demand. Both identities, therefore, are threatened. Longing and vulnerability become aggression, outrage. Tolerance is actually a matter of compromise, not of compulsory assent. Right may genuinely threaten right, without either being 'wrong'.

Purity and outrage

The process of identity assertion, dynamic as it is, is not uniform. Nor is it necessarily led by the march of progress. The pluralist liberties of modern cultural spaces act in ways that imitate the unregulated market more than they imitate the rules of a forum, competing for an attention share that will grant legitimacy through sheer noise. The automatic recourse to needs/rights-based claims therefore often depends upon dominating an implicit but inevitably inaccurate hierarchy of oppressions.

Yet, since some kinds of self-fashioning are in genuine collision with others, whose sense of identity is to be privileged, and whose subordinated? How should it be judged and who does the judging? Will it proceed in terms of relative need? Or in terms of relative right? Or simply in the name of choice? Will it be arbitrated by voices any more measured than the online cultural politics of purity and outrage? Not only are few asking such questions, but it becomes increasingly hard to find any dispassionate space in which they might be asked at all.

In the heavily contested areas of gender and sexuality, all identities compete for recognition. Norms are yardsticks for rebellion as well as for conformity. Sex and gender are powerful identity markers in a culture that has idolized sexual desire as ours has. And the culture wars over gender are still being played against hugely powerful constructions of 'masculine' and 'feminine' shaped by centuries of male agency. You only have to look at any of the images that dominate all our media. For generations now we have been surrounded by powerful paradigms of ferociously gendered beauty, presented in an overtly heterosexual frame and angled towards a – remarkably pitiless and enduring – male gaze. They preside over every identity decision we make. That includes those that defy them. No one is free.

Pictures of perfection

Aged 11, I gazed longingly at two images of a slim and beautiful female nude which appeared in a humorous 1970s annual, *The Goodies File*. Over the two images, the words 'YOU CAN HAVE'. Under each, two promises. For men: 'Someone like this'. For women: 'A body like this'. And I knew it was a joke – of sorts – but I wished, really wished, I could have a body like this. She was so very beautiful. I would never look like her. Becoming someone's possession seemed almost worth it.

These gendered forms, and particularly the consumable female image, against which both women and men cannot help but measure and define their worth, have changed across my adult lifetime. And although for the whole of it women's bodies have been impossibly slight and implicitly androgynous, during the 1990s (the decade during which I turned 30) the fashion industry favoured a fiercely reduced version of the feminine, one that reached its extreme with the cruelties of heroin chic. One of its most famous images is of the visibly starving woman gazing shadow-eyed and hopeless from the Accurist advert for an ornate silver watch. The watch is clasped across her upper arm because her wrist is too thin to hold it. The image and its caption, which invites her to add a bit of (silver, ticking) weight to her stick-figure, does not even bother to conceal the misogyny of the fashionable gaze.[12]

At the time this advert appeared I was having trouble managing either to eat or to read (both, in my mind, equally necessary for continuing life, both impossible). The advert's haunted-looking image, which seemed to be everywhere, expressed what seemed to me like a truth at the time: that there was nothing available for female identity beyond this ghostly, doomed compliance, this slow, obedient vanishment. I did find my way beyond this view, which now seems to me wicked rather than true, but, since I am not a natural rebel, and since this world made me, it took time.

Since those days, tastes have swung away from the andro-gynous and towards more gender-polarized forms, where male and female are signified through strong, muscular, exaggerated silhouettes: for women, impossibly slim midriffs, setting off voluptuous breasts and buttocks and thighs; for men, ridic-ulously developed chests and arms tapering to a tiny waist. It's easier now to find images of strong female agency (and of masculine humiliation, which really doesn't strike me as an advance; why is it a good thing in films when women punch men?) but their expression is stylized through unrealistic, cartoon-influenced – and essentially pornographic – physical paradigms. This makes life differently but seriously difficult for young men and women negotiating gender expectations now.

---

12 See www.adeevee.com/1998/10/accurist-solid-silver-ladies-watches-put-some-weight-on-print/ (accessed 10.01.2020).

Shame and humiliation over body shape, once mostly an issue for women, increasingly extends its reach to men as well. For children and adolescents it is of almost epidemic proportions.

A recent BBC documentary on the trolling and attempted suicide of the Little Mix singer Jesy Nelson shows someone attempting to manage a gendered self-fashioning that demands the impossible.[13] Driven first to despair by contemptuous online judgements upon her as 'fat', we see her on the other side of counselling and therapy trying to understand what kind of identity she might have apart from the constructions and projections imposed upon her. She and her mother look wistfully at pictures of her as a child, as if at a lost freedom. Her mother tries to suggest to her she doesn't need to wear so much make-up. Jesy pushes this away: 'I enjoy make-up, I like it. Most girls like make-up, Mum.' 'If I could have back my Jes as she was before,' says her mother to camera afterwards, 'I'd change it like *that*, not have X-Factor, not have any of that . . . I miss – *her*.'[14] Later, Jesy's new boyfriend comments wonderingly on what he is barred from knowing about her; although they sleep together and share every other intimacy, he is not allowed to see her with her hair wet, and has to look at an old picture on the fridge to see her face surrounded with a frizzy cloud rather than an artfully straightened waterfall of hair. Odder still, she will set her alarm for a time before daylight in order to mend her make-up before he wakes up. He has never seen her naked face. She has a self to fashion, and the investment is costly.

The performance demands of 'masculinity' and 'femininity' have not been dislodged by several generations' worth of challenge. If anything, it has hardened their outlines. Of course these gendered shapings are constructs, but then constructs (as any argument based on performative selves must concede) are not imaginary just because they are constructed. They compel

13 See www.bbc.co.uk/iplayer/episode/po7lsr4d/jesy-nelson-odd-one-out (accessed 10.01.2020).

14 See www.bbc.co.uk/iplayer/episode/po7lsr4d/jesy-nelson-odd-one-out, 6 mins 59–8 mins 6.

belief. They may compel despair: what they ask of us is so impossible, yet so difficult to see past.

The person who battles to dismantle social constructions of masculine and feminine and the person who performs and thus adapts them are making different, and arguably incompatible, attempts to wrestle with a monstrous dominance. It is scarcely surprising that the second-wave feminist and the trans woman will not necessarily see eye to eye, the former still struggling to break the paradigm through direct, external critique and refusal, the latter embracing a more internalized subversion in a form that can sometimes itself look eerily like compliance.

What young person would not be daunted by the implacably gendered world they encounter as they grow up? It is easy to imagine the young girl who feels that her essential being would be better protected in a body not defined as female, or the young boy who cannot imagine himself into a masculinity defined by the grinning cultural monsters he has had to accept as powerful since the day of his birth. It could all look pretty impossible for any child, aged 10, say, watching the watershed of puberty and the incessant, sexualized demands of the adult body come closer and closer. How to ward all that off? Considering the mixed, impossible and polarized messages we send out culturally in relation to gender, no wonder some people don't want to tangle with any of it and simply opt to refuse the package: male, female, the whole damn lot.

So when some Christian communities try to inscribe and fix 'essential' qualities of male and female – male leadership, female nurture, all the rest of it – and set up a theology around it, it looks remarkably like a version of the same old gendered oppressions that secular culture already imposes upon the development of its children, giving away their joy, comfort, health and physical confidence as necessary sacrifices to the monetization of desire. I don't suppose anyone 'means' to do harm. But given that we are all soaked in this toxic stuff from birth to the grave, there's no easy way out. Not for anyone. Quasi-separatist Christian cultures are no more immune than anybody else.

How did we get here? How did we become beings who believe implicitly in our capacity for self-shaping as the route to fulfilment – and yet at the same time seem not to trust the selves we fashion? We remain (perhaps fortunately) strangely unconvinced by our own hype, shifting, fearful, angry. We default to worshipping the apparent certainties of our commercial images of bodily desire even as we say that they are not to be taken seriously. It's a complicated story, but here is one possible thread contributing to the rise of the anxious, isolated, godlessly sovereign, uncertain, hungry self.

Testing the heart

Back in the sixteenth century, Greenblatt notes, in passing, that his objects of study exhibit a powerful theological unease with self-fashioning even as they rush towards it. Do self-fashioners forget that they are created beings – that they are 'creatures'? He quotes Augustine: 'Hands off yourself . . . try to build up yourself and you will build a ruin.'[15] He also notes that the many and various pious exhortations towards the fashioning of the self upon Christ's example are in conflict with this austere Augustinian view.

Greenblatt has gestured towards a very long-standing and basic collision in the Christian history of human becoming. This is the collision between creaturely helplessness and the deliberately acquired habits of the soul. Could virtuous selfhood be learnt from the outside in, through deliberate imitation? Or are the original flaw-lines of the fallen human creature so pervasive, so crippling, that the only means to restoration is through the miracle of grace?

The upheavals of the Reformation, as it played out for England and its new Church, exacerbated the tension between creaturely dependence and self-conscious effort for anyone who took the state of their soul seriously. (At that point just about everyone.) The first reformers recommended heartfelt

---

15 Quoted in Greenblatt, *Renaissance Self-Fashioning*, p. 2, but taken from Peter Brown, *Religion and Society in the Age of Augustine* (London: Faber and Faber, 1972), p. 30.

repentance in the light of the need for God's grace. This was their sole route to holiness, challenging the performed actions and habits of public piety. But that wasn't all. During Mary I's reign, in the mid-1550s, when those reformers had to rush off hurriedly to the Continent to save their skins, they went to Calvin's Geneva. And when they came back, at Elizabeth I's accession in 1558, they brought Calvin's Geneva with them. England became not just a Protestant but a Calvinist country. That same Calvinism would later also be exported to America via dissident Puritans in the seventeenth century.

For the early modern English Calvinist as she lived her life, the dominant question was whether she were 'elect': whether she had been from eternity damned or saved. This was not something you could test. Virtue was no sign of redemption; viciousness no bar to it. Everything lay in the completeness of the soul's faith in God's grace; and only the saved would manage it, a group already preordained to have been granted faith and likely to be unconscious of who they were. (Consciousness of being 'saved' could, of course, itself be a sign of the wicked soul's self-deceit. Or not.)

This was extremely uncomfortable. People started going in for cycles of anxious self-examination. What did their faith really look like? Was it good enough? How would they know? Calvinism put the practices and disciplines of the holy life into a very odd category: they were necessary, for sure, but they were absolutely not sufficient. They might be hollow. No matter how ascetic you were, were you also *sincere*? Were you fooling yourself? Practice could not make perfect. The longing of your heart for God was under constant testing, and the testing process led more readily towards despair and exhaustion than towards relief.

So people found they needed, really needed, some guarantee, however provisional, of redemption. Practices of self-examination emerged, taking the heart to the depths of sorrow in order that it might emerge 'converted', utterly changed. Usually conversion was affirmed by a group of people who had emerged 'assured' from the same process as well as by the emotional outcome of the internal voyage. The journeys of the individual soul's life began to appear in journal form, narrating the struggle for a saving faith, and in the process hollowing out a larger and larger space for an internal being called the 'self' which journeyed ever more self-consciously towards knowing its pre-existent validation as good. (Or sometimes, for some unfortunates, as damned, a journey tending to end in suicide.[16]) These literary forms shaped and grew into the profoundly important genre of the novel.

And, for modern understandings of identity, all that is really, really important. The sense of self as we live it now has been shaped in part by a process that is internal but also anxiously cyclical, a matter of unprovable personal perception. The philosopher Charles Taylor talks about the 'porous' self of the pre-Reformation person becoming a 'buffered' one, a construction with impermeable walls, where the self validated its own decisions about what to believe and the outer world of collectively formed beliefs had much less power.[17] That's what we inherit: modern selves are 'buffered', walled away from certainty by endless loops of self-reference.

We have received, then, from our Calvinist forebears a dreadful contradiction about the nature of belief. It seems as if the grounds for belief are *there*, all right, but forever out of reach, fixed as a truth beyond the point where human efforts of will or understanding could ever reach them, immutable and yet silent. But at the same time *belief itself*, authentically reached through the testing of the heart, seems to beckon towards self-fulfilment by allowing access to this unreachable truth. Only it doesn't, because the heart cannot settle or still itself upon its object, yearning continually for a divine assurance which then manifests as another form of unattained yearning

---

16 As in the bestselling account of the despair of Francis Spira. Nathaniel Bacon, *A Relation of the Fearful Estate of Francis Spira* (1548).

17 Charles Taylor discusses this in his influential *A Secular Age* (Cambridge, MA: Belknap Press, 2007), but gives a very helpful summary here: https://tif.ssrc.org/2008/09/02/buffered-and-porous-selves/ (accessed 10.01.2020).

which might or might not contain that assurance. Once in that cycle, how could you ever stop?

Performing who you are

So people turned to another, older model of virtue: the performed self. As reform hollowed out the new, internalized yet deeply doubtful space called 'self' in the human mind, meeting the need for self-conscious self-examination, people filled it up with the surer habits of self-fashioning. They began to use the disciplines of habit to fix that new internal space, to *perform* who they were. They inscribed character upon themselves through constant repeated practices. And it didn't just play out in piety, because piety was still bound into everything everyone did. It played out *everywhere*.

The rising world of the sixteenth-century theatre provided a complete and ready-made metaphor for the project of performed identity. 'All the world's a stage/ And all the men and women merely players', the melancholy Jaques observed in Shakespeare's *As You Like It*.[18] The comparison was an ever-recurring cliché, its power deriving from its circularity: the real with the fictive, the fictive with the real. Was it that the world was a site of performance, endlessly making its truth, every player upon it acting a part that constructed a reality? 'This is my play's last scene,' wrote John Donne of an imagined deathbed, without any hint of a sense that such an image denoted something contrived, fictive or untrue; and indeed the account we have of his actual deathbed suggests that he performed its meaning with terrifying, theatrical completeness.[19] Or was it that the metaphor exposed

---

18 William Shakespeare, *As You Like It*, II.7.139–40, in *As You Like It*, ed. Agnes Latham (Walton-on-Thames: Methuen & Co. Ltd, 1975), pp. 55–6.

19 John Donne, 'Holy Sonnet 3', in *The Oxford Authors: John Donne*, ed. John Carey (Oxford: Oxford University Press, 1990), p. 174; Izaak Walton, *Life of Donne* (1640), in *Izaak Walton: Selected Writings*, ed. Jessica Martin (Manchester: Carcanet Press, 1997), esp. pp. 55–70.

the fictive nature of such a performance, drawing attention to a different mode of reality under clothes, gesture, donned selves? Donne, in another mood, spent some time pointing out that a terrified deathbed, a failure of performance, had no moral or salvific significance: 'we have no . . . art to give a presagition of spiritual death and damnation upon any such indication as we see in any dying man'; and a contemporary preacher agreed with him that you could read nothing from behaviour, even if some-one showed 'an appearance of anguish or perplexity, or even a kind of despair in their death'.[20]

The Pauline epistles, rich source for the self-examination of the soul, provide a helpful metaphor for effective and properly creaturely self-performance: the metaphor of the spiritually clothed soul. 'Put ye on the Lord Jesus Christ,' writes Paul to the Romans; and he elaborates the metaphor elsewhere.[21] A 'faithful man', according to the spiritual writer Joseph Hall, 'when he goes in to converse with God, wears not his own Clothes, but takes them still out of the rich Wardrobe of his Redeemer'.[22] But Hall's use of Paul's metaphor also destabilized it – clothing kept in a 'Wardrobe' is not only for putting on but for taking off, and introduces the possibility of shifting identity, part-time Christlikeness.

Writers began to explore the burgeoning character of the 'hypocrite': the 'actor' in borrowed dress, whose persona con-cealed a different and disgraceful truth. 'Hypocrisy,' wrote Milton in *Paradise Lost*, 'the only evil that walks/ Invisible,

20 John Donne, *Deaths Duell, or, a Consolation to the Soul, against the Dying Life, or the Living Death of the Body* (1632), in http:// public-library.uk/ebooks/27/18.pdf, pp. 5–6 (accessed 10.01.2020); 'Peace in Death, or the Quiet End of the Righteous', in *Threnoikos: The House of Mourning*, ed. Daniel Featley (London, 1640), pp. 684–5.

21 Romans 13.14 (in the translation of 1611). See also Colossians 3.12–14; Galatians 3.27.

22 Joseph Hall, *Characters of Vertues and Vices* (London, 1608), p. 20.

except to God alone.'[23] Was any person what he seemed? Not only to the outer world, but even to each individual, the truth of the self seemed impossible to pin down.

'Oh to vex me, contraries meet in one,' wrote John Donne. 'I change in vows, and in devotion.' And then he shrugged his shoulders and headed for an interim, and distinctly Pauline, paradox:

> Inconstancy unnaturally hath begot
> A constant habit.[24]

'Contraries meet in one'

Now take God out of the mix. Remove this notion of dynamic yet stable personhood whose creative qualities endow creatures with a shared meaning, and have a look at what is left. By this time the self is the only object of search. Its 'truth' is apparently to be found through the project of self-fashioning – and at the same time through endlessly receding self-interrogation.

So we are invited to discover authenticity both in performing and in distrusting our own performance; both in donning habits and in perceiving them as nothing but covers for some other concealment; both in stating the self as immutably discovered and as an endlessly shifting and flickering process of constant change eventually plummeting towards decay. These are not paradoxes. They are violent collisions. No one can stand such psychic violence for long; it's as unendurable as the Calvinist doubt of our ancestors, but without even the hint of spiritual rescue.

Secular theories of the self notice how fragile the construct is, how mutable. Some make a feature of its mutability – think

---

23 John Milton, *Paradise Lost*, III.682–3, in *The Poetical Works of John Milton*, ed. Helen Darbishire (London: Oxford University Press, 1958), p. 70.

24 John Donne, 'Holy Sonnet 19', in *The Oxford Authors: John Donne*, ed. Carey, p. 288; Romans 7.19.

of the 1990s fuss about 'postmodernity' – but given that self-hood is basic to how we tell ourselves and our children who we are, its playful deconstruction plays a very risky game indeed with what we euphemistically call 'mental health'.

'Open and honest'

During the time when I was growing up, self-interrogation, truth-search, was dominant. Nothing was more important than 'sincerity'. Spontaneity guaranteed a kind of authority. The journeys of self-discovery were the dominant spiritual form. And if desire altered with time and circumstance – as you 'fell out of love', for example – the truth of the self demanded that you follow where it led, out of the old relationship, into the new; out of the old sexuality, into the new; out of the old, tired, understandings of religion as stability and never-mind-how-you-feel-today and into the new give-me-something-to-feel. Baby-boom prosperity (and I was born at the very tail end of that generation, two decades after the end of World War Two) fed into that vision with a kind of infernal neatness. The truth of the self, constructed to be 'authentic', played into the project of consumerism, of throwaway histories, of relationships with built-in obsolescence, with uncanny ease.

Hypocrisy was the ultimate twentieth-century sin, as spontaneity was its primary virtue. Hypocrisy is still a word with great power, but it has been whipped out of private discourse and into corporatespeak, since no larger shared principles than the boundaries of a business ethic now exist. The demands of spontaneity as a *mode* require selves to be performed within genres at every level of social interaction (for example on personal social media) in ways that are by any standards 'hypocritical' because they cannot and should not disclose everything.[25] This is both necessary and implicitly transgressive.

---

25 This is a social media commonplace. In the 2017 remake of the 1995 children's film *Jumanji*, we watch a teenage girl spend several minutes setting up an elaborate staging of spontaneous charm for her phone camera, which she posts under the hashtag '#unfiltered life'.

We employ the dominant cliché of 'transparency' in what we demand of organizations and individuals, a metaphor that imagines communal transactions as glassy, in one sense invisible, something to look *through* rather than at, towards not only the outcomes but the motives and processes of every potentially slippery decision. Social programming of different kinds – within schools, workplaces, governmental welfare regulators such as social workers – use the doublet 'open and honest' to describe the ideal form of person-to-person transaction, employing the fiction that only the guilty ever have anything to keep to themselves. 'Private' settings on computers are set up to look furtive: dark, non-disclosing backgrounds to screens – because, presumably, there's no category of human privacy between doing something disgraceful and being content to be monetized by huge corporations. Everyone is on film.

Don't find yourself: create yourself

It doesn't take much looking to see the individualist search for personal happiness as by now almost entirely possessed by the consumerist cycle. Throwaway relationships follow from throwaway selves in a culture that strains always towards acquisition, expansion, towards expressions of an increasingly bloated and unhappy selfhood on a planet becoming sicker and sicker from its own exploitation. And the spendthrift luxuries of throwaway performance look more troubling, more destructive and more pervasive now than they have ever done in my lifetime. The 'spontaneous' politician who performs honesty with an absolute disregard for consistency or truth, as the need or greed of the moment requires, heads up policy decisions for the wider world in both the UK and the USA. Self-belief, performed with conviction, has more authority than sober fact, and commands more trust.

On the smaller scale of ordinary citizens, people are investing a good deal of faith in the power of the performed self. The authenticities of performance are taken extremely seriously: these fashioned selves are, for as long as they last, the only reality on offer. 'Don't find yourself, create yourself' is a popular meme. Identifying absolutely with the demands of a particular desire may be followed by an equally absolute identification with a contrasting persona: the detachment required for self-regulating who you think you might be over a span of time where you might feel rather a lot of different and contrasting things is not a valued skill. At the same time, depression and self-harm rise and rise.

The implicit – and sometimes explicit – assumption by which we live is that the human person is only a kind of template, malleable to a mixture of will, effort and expense: there only to be wrought into more desired and expedient forms. The dominant metaphor for thinking about embodied personhood is the machine, complex yet programmable (though slower and more erratic than actual complex programmable machines). This is the same metaphor the perhaps suicidal Hamlet used of his own body when he signed himself 'yours, while this machine is to him' in the Shakespeare play bearing his name.[26] In 1600 the expression was a way of expressing an unusual self-alienation. The metaphor has now become a commonplace, the self-alienation an everyday experience.

Often bodily nature and personhood are seen as semi-detached. The body is a malleable idea rather than present or material, especially when so much communication is online. Avatars and assertions are deemed to offer truths not visible on the backward, stubborn, rebellious flesh. And with the metaphysical self there is no need for unitary identity; you can be an array of different people under different handles for different purposes. Or you can change swiftly as part of the fluidity of being; change names, qualities, interests, emotional focus, principles. Like a modern novel, a modern self need have no point; need not distinguish between significant and insignificant experience; can be as episodic as it wants; need have no epiphany, no discovery, no revelation; may chart constant change or no

---

26 William Shakespeare, *Hamlet*, II.2.130 (1603), in *Hamlet: Prince of Denmark*, ed. Philip Edwards (Cambridge: Cambridge University Press, 1985), p. 124.

change at all; may have no cadence, no ending, no beginning, no obvious order, no significant or lasting relationships; need learn nothing beyond the fragmented accumulation of sensation. It sounds like freedom; actually it's about as free, and about as safe, as driving a car very fast on a crowded road.

The selves that trust their own fashioning tend to be very responsive to this generation's strong, exaggerated constructions of masculinity and femininity, either in conformity or in rebellion. They recognize that the demands such constructions make are high. Body sculpting, from the less interventionist kinds based on exercise to the more invasive kinds based on drugs and surgery, are commonplace. Cosmetic skill is highly valued. Online faking possibilities make physical reality disappointing. Children as they grow up are increasingly likely to measure themselves against unrealistic expectations of what they could look like, or could attain, or even could be. People are unmerciful to each other's self-creations, searching for flaws, inconsistencies, signs of disguise. And, of course, they find them.

The limits to performance

Yet people are not machines. We don't actually have the last say over what happens to our feelings. We are profoundly affected by experience, not merely the makers of it. Our lives are full of things we haven't made or chosen – closings-down, or life-changing perceptions as well as sickness, death, childbirth, age. You will be changed without meaning it or wanting it. That is both the danger and the redemptive opportunity for the buffered self. We are, by the mercy of God, not in complete control. Things may happen to the mind and heart that are like *reminders*, recognitions, that seem to encapsulate meaning in spite of all perverse efforts of will or reasoning or desire. The message might be news of a far country, or it might be news of home.

It might even be that we are more unified beings either than we fear or than we behave; and that this is good news.

The gift of the soul

I do not know quite what 'the soul' is. Or, rather, it is for me a word that contains a profound meaning with some powerful mystery to it. I treat it rather as I used to treat complex words I found in the marvellous process of learning to read fluently, where I could see how to use them but would have been a bit stumped to offer a definition. Such words unfolded their meaning subtly, multifariously, in the work they actually did, rather than functionally in a bald and bounded description of the work they were supposed to do.

In my profession as priest, the word 'soul' has a vocational significance. When I was licensed to my first parish, the bishop, on giving me my licence, said: 'Receive the cure of souls, which is both yours and mine.' The 'cure' or 'care' (the words are closely associated) I took on with the promises I then made was to the living and yet transcendent essence of the people I would serve, an essence called 'soul'. It was associated both with the life-giving breath maintaining their bodies (and so with the often tangled stories of their lives), and also with the breathing of God's creative powers in sustaining their person-hood outside the rule of time.

Those souls, as they lived in the world, were not immutable, though. They needed 'care'. Within a faith – the Christian gospel – that has healing close to its centre, I could see that they, like me, also needed the Lord's 'cure'. The cure of the soul was God's good news for people in their being and in their becom-ing. I knew such cures existed; that God found messy, surprising and counter-intuitive ways to invite people to become whole.

I knew this because once upon a time my own soul received cure. I knew both what it felt like to be losing my soul, and what it felt like to be given it back again. And while I was blindly collusive in the process of soul-loss, its restoration came out of the blue, without any sense of my own volition and control.

In my mid-twenties, in the depths of a physically violent and controlling sexual relationship, I began rapidly to lose ordinary qualities I was used to possessing. First, I started to forget how to drive a car. I hadn't known how to drive for very long, in fact, so that loss of confidence didn't seem tremendously surprising. But then something much worse happened. I forgot how to spell.

I have always been able to spell. From the day I started to read, aged 4, when my father showed me the words in a *Dr Seuss Dictionary* as I sat on his knee, I could spell any word I saw after reading it once. Being able to spell was deeply embedded in the person I knew I was. Spelling tests at school were pleasures, though also a bit pointless. I didn't remember the words. I just saw them. But at this stage in my life, constantly fearful and more tired than I have ever been before or since, I couldn't see them any more. I think it's probably not an exaggeration to say that I was more frightened by forgetting how to spell than I was by the possibility that I might be seriously hurt or killed. I thought about the danger I might be in sometimes, but from a dreamlike distance, a problem for some other day. I was developing a habit of daydreams in which my partner rescued me from his own violence and I leaned on him gratefully for the rescue. This did not strike me as strange. But I worried about my illiteracy.

Then during a very bad moment on a very bad evening, a bright picture took me over. I ceased briefly to be where I was or inside what was happening to me. I found myself instead utterly detached from place and time, running barefoot down a grassy slope. The grass was wet. I was wearing a new red dress my mother made for me, and I was running for the joy of running, the joy of the new dress, the slope of the garden, the flash and gleam of light on the drops in the grass. I was filled with that joy. It was a memory, of course, not a vision, a memory of a moment in my own past, but extraordinarily powerful; and it stayed with me, a shining presence I had forgotten. It was a gift from I knew not where.

I lost my blankness of spirit. I made, within a few days, first steps towards freedom and safety: stole the car keys one evening, taking advantage of his drunken sleep, and left quietly with my feverish 7-year-old wrapped in a quilt in my arms and two plastic bags, one of randomly chosen clothes and some Calpol, the other containing my PhD thesis notes.

I drove – perfectly competently – to a temporary safety, to the one woman of my acquaintance who had noticed what was happening and quietly offered help when I was ready.

It was, of course, only the beginning of a long process with its own terrors, and it involved a very long slog, years' worth of it, towards any kind of decent or viable daily life; but I never went back. I had not chosen to remember my self, to come into my right mind, any more than I had been in control of the loss of my abilities to spell or to drive. It was soul-cure, healing.

To find redemption in the breaking of a relationship seems like a strange move in a book that tries to point towards fidelity in sexual love. The more so in that this was a relationship that had taken all my attention and shaped my understanding of desire from my early teens, so that in a neat world it should have been the one to receive a lifetime of that attention from me. But I was wrong ever to try to think so, and I knew I was wrong, and trying to make it work was one of the wrongest things I have ever done. Sometimes the command is to break those bonds that make slaves of everyone involved.

I was so slow to notice this with my whole attention that I needed to be shown it. I didn't re-estimate the value of my own being, because I had forgotten it. I am enduringly grateful to be shown something I couldn't find by myself. And I notice that the shifts in my own spirit at other times in my life have also been outside my own control: discoveries that appear apparently outside my will or decision; showings (put the word into Greek and you get *epiphany*) that alter and intensify meaning. My ability to be thankful, or even to make meaningful sense of my life, depends upon all those things shown me that I do not control, cannot will into being. I am glad to be a creature who worships God and waits for the light to spring up; and not to be a lonely god myself in an unendurable state of self-creation.

I do not ask whether I have a soul. I know she is there, held in the gaze of God's love, beautifully independent of what I might ever decide to do, or to be, or even to know. The day I forget who I am altogether she will still be there, running in the sunlight and the dew in a red dress down the green hill.

PART 3

Holiness

*Which imagines ways to live holy lives
within the shaping constraints of the modern world*

6

Converting

Going home

Jesus has a habit of sending people home. Across the Gospels of Mark and Luke are a scatter of encounters with the same pattern. Jesus meets and has a short conversation with someone in trouble, sickness, grief or torment of mind (often also with the people who love and care for them), discovers what they want, and makes the change they need to live whole and well within the relationships they already have. Sometimes they ask to follow him, sometimes they don't. But even for the ones who do, such as the man healed of multiple divisive agonies of the soul and restored 'to his right mind', who 'begged'[1] to be with him, Jesus' message is clear. He 'sent him away, saying, "Return to your home, and declare how much God has done for you."'[2]

One of the earliest of these encounters, with the paralytic who longs to walk again, has the command to go home embedded in the very words of healing: 'I say to you, stand up, take up your mat and go to your home.'[3] It's a particularly striking encounter in that the words Jesus speaks both about and to this particular man are not just about his physical impairment, but about the condition of his whole being, the health of soul and body together: 'Son, your sins are forgiven.'[4]

---

1 Mark 5.18.
2 Luke 8.38–39, but also Mark 5.18–19.
3 Mark 2.11; Luke 5.24–25.
4 Mark 2.5; Luke 5.20.

'Go in peace,' says Jesus to the woman he heals of a persistent haemorrhage.[5] He reminds the family of a child he restores to life that she needs their domestic comfort and nurture: 'give her something to eat'.[6] He sends a woman home to her small daughter, the child already freed from mental pain and 'lying on the bed'[7] waiting for her mother's return. A centurion finds health restored to his valued servant back home: he never even meets Jesus in person, but he trusts his power to mend things within the order and relationships of his household.[8] When Jesus encounters a grief-stricken woman, alone and desolate in the world, whose son has died, he raises the young man from death: 'Young man, I say to you, rise!' As the man begins to speak, Jesus interrupts his words to remind him of the responsibilities of love: he 'gave him to his mother'.[9] A boy, an only child, racked by fits, when he is healed is restored to where he should be: Jesus 'gave him back to his father'.[10] A blind man brought to him by friends in the town of Bethsaida is sent back home, independent, looking 'intently' and seeing 'everything clearly'. Don't be distracted now, says Jesus, 'Do not even go into the village.'[11] Go home.

And Zacchaeus, the rich tax collector, socially hated, socially predatory, goes out one day and climbs a tree in order to try and see what holiness looks like; to 'see who Jesus was'. He finds himself entertaining God at his own table. 'When Jesus came to the place, he looked up and said to him, "Zacchaeus, hurry up and come down; for I must stay at your house today."' Zacchaeus is eager. He 'hurried down and was happy to welcome him'. The shared meal at his home is only the beginning, though. Zacchaeus sees something he has not seen before: that his relationships with those around him are distorted and damaged by his mode of life, and that to be restored he himself

5 Mark 5.34; Luke 8.48.
6 Mark 5.43; Luke 8.55.
7 Mark 7.30.
8 Luke 7.2–10.
9 Luke 7.11–17.
10 Luke 9.42.
11 Mark 8.22–26.

must restore that balance and mend those relationships. So he 'stood there and said . . . "Look, half of my possessions, Lord, I will give to the poor; and if I have defrauded anyone of anything, I will pay back four times as much."' And Jesus sees 'salvation' in this, because Zacchaeus has remembered that where he belongs is what matters, and has noticed that the acquisition of goods is hurting his identity, his essential being, by hurting the relationships that make him: 'he too is a son of Abraham,' says Jesus.[12]

Resurrection as homecoming

The most violent of partings points towards home. At the empty tomb, the disciples' desolation is interrupted by a messenger who tells them that they are looking for him in the wrong place. 'He has been raised; he is not here.' Go home. 'He is going ahead of you to Galilee; there you will see him, just as he told you.'[13] Mary Magdalene recognizes her beloved when he speaks her name: she is brought home to herself as surely as the day he gave her back her right mind.[14] Thomas' agonized disbelief in Jesus' risen life becomes recognition, a relationship painfully restored through touch. The joining of hand to wound brings together a metaphysical and a physical understanding of reality. It mends Thomas' bitter grief, shows him a truth he had not seen clearly before. 'My Lord and my God!'[15]

Almost the very last sight of Jesus in the Gospel of John is a homecoming. He stands on the Galilee shore to welcome those who love him, local men coming back to land disappointed after a dark and fruitless night. His presence changes their condition from empty to overjoyed, their nets whole and full with the weight of the fish. He cooks them breakfast, eats with them the food he gave and prepared, mending into completion not

---

12 Luke 19.2–10.
13 Mark 16.6–7; also Matthew 28.5–7.
14 John 20.16; Luke 8.2.
15 John 20.24–29.

only their violent parting but the betrayal that is damaging Peter's soul.[16]

'Where you do not wish to go'

To go home is not to stay the same. To convert his life Peter must turn full circle. He will leave that encounter on his familiar shore for ever changed. He has learnt something about the nature of love: that in the choice of it he chooses unexpected constraint. To be made whole is to accept the unknown, to lose the control you thought you had upon the conditions of your being. 'Do you love me?' asks Jesus. The question seems to Peter unnecessary; to have it asked of him three times (one time for each past betrayal) maddening. 'Lord, you know everything,' he points out irritably. 'You know that I love you.'

Well, yes, Jesus agrees, I do know, but I wonder if you understand what love demands and where it must go. Once you've opted for the bonds of love, your life, the wholeness of it that we have breathing between us, is no longer just your own. It's not even mainly your own. It belongs to love. So, 'Feed my sheep'. And then he tells him something else:

> Very truly I tell you, when you were younger, you used to fasten your own belt, and to go wherever you wished. But when you grow old, you will stretch out your hands, and someone else will fasten a belt around you and take you where you do not wish to go.

The Gospel-writer – never one to miss an explanatory opportunity – adds an aside: '(He said this to indicate the kind of death by which he would glorify God.)' And, of course, he's right. These are words that conclude a kind of revelation for Peter over the course of that morning. Jesus is saying to him something like this. The pattern of your life, of which your betrayals were a part, leads now to your steadfastness. The

---

16 John 21.4-19.

steadfastness love finds in your restoration to wholeness will see you always close to me, standing with me in my place, both for pain and loss and for the eventual homecoming that I embody and express. My promise is that the final violence, the last tearing away, will bring you home.

The evangelist was thinking of Peter's martyrdom. But they are words for any last struggle. I last heard them spoken aloud by my father, from memory, as he was dying in the spring of 2019. 'That's where I am now,' he said. 'Being taken where I do not wish to go.' His smile was amused, conspiratorial. The hubris of comparing his ordinary deathbed to the martyrdom of St Peter was a joke worth sharing. But he was also making a clear, wry reference to the everyday indignities that had become the conditions of his life, finding an indirect way of looking towards their inevitable end, and – typical of his unflinchingness and of his emotional reticence – holding tacitly to a divine promise without evading its pain. He made his death, helpless, content to be held by the heart of his family, a man who had in his youth striven to outstrip us all, ambivalent about the bonds of love, striding impossibly ahead on every Sunday walk, driving hour after hour across the roads of Europe with his weary family squashed in the back, always looking for something or other that would not come into focus, endlessly impatient, always restless for elsewhere. But it wasn't elsewhere he needed. Go home.

My own perverse twenties, turning away from family, friends, insufficiently attentive to my child's need, frantic to get this one intensely distorted relationship right whatever else I ditched in the process, and suddenly reminded of who I was, where I came from, what I owed to the webs of love that made me. Go home.

Stability

There is a very visible other side to the Gospels (especially noticeable in the Gospel of Matthew), which uses the language of discipleship, of travelling, even wandering, of being not at home in the world. Such language is prominent in the discourses of the Church. Baptism is characterized in its liturgy as joining 'Christ's pilgrim people'.[17] Multiple 'journey' references (the 'journey of discipleship', for example) within churchspeak have moved from being frequent cliché into that settled dead place almost beyond metaphor.

And it's true that Jesus' call, 'Follow me', the call he made to the disciples, which is therefore seen as paradigmatic of all calls to faithfulness, occurs in the Gospels at least as often as he tells people to go home. He praises those who leave 'houses or brothers or sisters or father or mother or children or fields',[18] and responds ambiguously rather than understandingly to the request of the man who asks whether he might first bury his father.[19] This seems to make him markedly less tolerant than the prophet Elijah in this one respect.[20] The instructions to the disciples in the tenth chapter of Luke emphasize how important it is to travel light, and imply a vocation that is always on the move. Jesus remarks of himself, 'the Son of Man has nowhere to lay his head'.[21] All this is a very real part of the command to sit light to the world's claims in obedient attentiveness to the demands of God's love. All the homes from which we come, all the homes to which we return, are themselves temporary refuges, way-stations towards the first and last home for the soul in communion with its maker, redeemer, sustainer.

That acknowledged, I wonder whether the Church's continual metaphorical emphasis on restless travel helps much with our understanding of the responsibilities of love. In some ways the trope of pilgrimage fits all too easily both with a world of zero-hours contracts and with the secular clichés of abandoned serial commitments: 'put a line under it'; 'time to move on'. It chimes with lives in which jobs, relationships, homes, are

17 'Holy Baptism', *Common Worship: Christian Initiation* (London: Church House Publishing, 2006).
18 Matthew 19.29.
19 Matthew 8.21; Luke 9.59.
20 1 Kings 19.19–21, where Elijah tacitly allows his successor Elisha to say goodbye to his parents before following him.
21 Matthew 8.20.

all temporary expedients, a world impatient with rootedness and structurally unhelpful for making lifelong commitment, whether to place or to people or to vocation. But it isn't always time to move on. To be whole, people need to make some kind of unitary sense of history and memory. Somehow we only seem to know that in relation to retrospective talking therapies rather than in the attention we pay to our lives and relationships as they are actually happening. The project of fidelity is so important that it's worth holding on to even in the face of its difficulty and frequent failure. That's especially true within the Christian vocation that prizes faithfulness even as it recognizes the need for forgiveness in the betrayals of love.

Those encounters with Jesus in Mark and Luke, which form a large part of what is often called the 'healing miracles', are not trivial, also-ran extras to a dominant narrative about leaving human love behind in the long journey towards salvation. Jesus' encounters with the sick and sorrowful are not done to be pieces of attention-grabbing power display – quite the reverse. Jesus nearly always begs those healed not to talk of it. Nor are they a foolish, doomed attempt to reorder the world's relationships person by person. They are expressions of compassion, and they are 'signs', as Jesus says, pictures of the coming kingdom of love. They show what God's work in the world looks like. It looks very much like learning to love well where you already are.

In the Gospel of John, the verb most associated with the Spirit's presence is the word 'abide' (*menō*) – sometimes also translated by an older English word for deep-rooted living: 'dwell'. In the same Gospel, Jesus joins divine homecoming with the actions of love and fidelity when he speaks to the disciples before his arrest and betrayal: 'Those who love me will keep my word, and my Father will love them, and we will come to them and make our home with them.'[22]

Time after time in the Gospels, someone gets their life back, and the very next thing they are told to do is to go home. Join up your relationships, says Jesus. Take your part again where

---

22 John 14.23.

you are making your life, and make it a good one. Tell everyone what God has done for you. Since you were made whole
your life's work is reconciliation, faithfulness to the burdens
you already carry, spreading out not only into your history and
your ability to live with yourself but into your dealings with
every person whose life you touch.

Obedience as freedom

Towards the beginning of the history of the Christian faith,
a man who had never met Jesus had a change of heart. He
was a devout Jew, and temperamentally he was a systematizer,
a pattern-maker. He worshipped God. He was clever, rhetor-
ically inventive, something of a visionary. He was a natural
leader. He knew where he belonged and he knew the extent of
his own powers. His name was Saul.

He loathed the messy trail left by the followers of what they
called 'the Way', by the inconsistent jumble of sayings and
stories about the rabbi Jesus. He was annoyed and outraged by
the extravagant promises of their resurrection story, by their
appropriation of the messianic tradition, and by the hints of
universal, worldwide promise they drew provocatively out of
the original clear narrative of the chosen people of Israel. The
whole thing needed stamping out, for everyone's sake, before it
caused both political and religious instability. And he travelled
towards the city of Damascus on his self-appointed (and so far
rather successful) task to do exactly that.

Something happened to him on the way. A light took away
his sight; a voice took away his certainties. 'I am Jesus, who
you are persecuting.' The voice spoke to command his obedience. 'But get up and enter the city, and you will be told
what you are to do.'[23] From being a leader, he had to become
helpless, from a visionary to become one without vision, his
hands held, guided by others into the city to which he had
travelled with such sure authority. Once there, his healing was

---

23 Acts 9.5–6.

brought about when both he and a follower of the Way called Ananias obeyed a command to trust a man they knew should be a dangerous enemy. For Ananias, that man was Saul himself. God asked Ananias to believe that Saul was to be *turned around*; no longer a violent persecutor of Jesus' Way but now a man dedicated to the experience of suffering for Jesus' sake. For Saul himself, Ananias, a representative of the very heretical group he had sworn to eliminate in the name of God, had to become instead the herald of divine healing. These two, as they met, relinquished control, listening attentively to God bespeaking their mutual change of heart. What followed was sight, and wholeness of being, and the renewals of baptism – and, much further down the line, the worldwide community of believers in the good news of Jesus we call 'the Church'.

Saul's name changed to Paul. He 'regained his strength'. He was still the same person: still recognizably a systematizer, still the bossy, subtle, devious, stubborn visionary he had been before – but turned around, converted, attentively obedient to a power that was not his own. Like Peter – also renamed, also promised the suffering that goes with relinquishing personal control – Paul had learnt the fundamental lesson of the nature of love: that to choose love was to choose constraint as well as joy.

Conversion of life

For many, perhaps most people, it's not immediately clear what 'going home' might mean or look like. Few get their 'road to Damascus' moment in some clear and unambiguous form. Love demands that we find a meaning beyond ourselves and the incessant noise of our clamouring wants and deafened wills: that we find a way to listen to the voice of God and notice how much it is *not* an echo of the self. It asks us to pay sustained attention to the thread of truth that speaks within and sometimes across our modes of life.

Yet alignment to the divine choice won't necessarily conform to some neat behavioural template. Nothing in the Word of God says that holiness of life looks like the 'Peter and Jane' picture of mummy, daddy, two lovely children and a dog living in their nice detached house with its green, green lawn. For some fidelity will be like that. For many others the command to faithful living will look different indeed.

What happens, stays happened. Conversion means that people change their direction, not their character or their history. Desire, that constant reminder that there is something beckoning beyond any immediate horizon, is there to be re-purposed: it is not there to be torn out or thrown away or violently bent out of shape. The flowering of desire in the human soul is a herald for God's presence, because desire points towards something we have not made for ourselves and cannot encompass. It speaks God's truth: that the perfectly regulated and performed self is not, in fact, available to anyone. Neither the religious nor the secular closed self can thrive.

For those who recognize that they are *dependent* animals – creatures – this is not such a terrible shock. There are cracks in the persona through which the Spirit can shine, breathe, knock. Responding to the light, the voice, the invitation, will be a choice that brings with it the constraints of obedience, the complicated demands of connection.

Holiness of life

Were we serious about proclaiming Jesus' invitation to be made whole, rather than mistaking respectability for holiness, our churches would inevitably contain many more people who brought with them the mess that attends the modern experience of radically discontinuous lives, generations' worth of them. People with hugely different contexts and life-histories from each another, yes, but also discontinuous within themselves, the products of multiple different households, caregivers, geographical locations, identities. They would bring along with them the usual tangled mass of relationships, some in bad shape, some dead except in their enduring emotional impact, some limping along, some destructive or conflicted or furious or needy, some managing somehow – perhaps unexpectedly, or in unexpected family shapes – to thrive.

Everyone alive now has grown up with the compensatory low-grade commercial seductions that go with the incessant monetization of human desire. These seductions have set out to undermine (in passing, not in malice) the projects of fidelity, kindness, understanding, sustained attention, self-discipline and self-knowledge, because dissatisfaction, outrage, a short attention span and emotional incontinence make sales, and contentment doesn't. Sticking with what you've got, preferring to mend rather than to discard: these are not decisions to be encouraged, speaking in economic terms – not even in the face of a planet in environmental crisis.

People in their millions gallantly resist the relentless messages to stay miserable, insecure and cross, but resisting them also takes its toll. They get tired and discouraged. Love, faith and confidence (a word that is about trust in self and others) are at a huge disadvantage. Add to that the continual instability of the modern state, its unaffordable houses, its insecure jobs, its chronically underfunded schools and civic resources and healthcare, its savagery with the weak, the disabled and the powerless, and stability looks like a kind of impossible dream. (Perhaps, even, a dream you might think only money, a *lot* of money, could buy. And there is no doubt that money helps in a world revolving round money.) And yet, in spite of everything, kindness, generosity, commitment, self-sacrifice all flower in our difficult and barren soil.

Consider for a moment an outrageous fantasy. Say some cultural switch got thrown for some inexplicable reason and people were flocking to the churches. In such a case, the 'conversion of life' asked of this unexpected mass of new worshippers would be deeply countercultural, because it would start by asking what fidelity might look like in the relationships *they already had*. In mending, not discarding; in sticking with things and people and places and commitments. What would it mean to say to millions of restless people, 'Go home'?

To go home would be to face some hard questions. What kind of courage – and what kind of humility – would it take to look with an unflinching and unsentimental eye at the relationships I already have? To understand the interwoven needs and inabilities and failures of care that might be part of them? To discern what are the demands of love, and what might be some other less admirable or generous bond? Deliberately to shoulder the burdens of fidelity, asking: what do my children need? What do the frail in my family need? What space is there for mutual attention, for reconciliation, for the living curiosity to discover why things aren't going well? When am I being selfish, or self-involved? Are there actions or habits of mind for which I should ask forgiveness? Are there some things over which I genuinely have no power, and how well do I live with them? What do I need to change? Are any of my relationships destructive, violent? Am I really owed as much as I think by life? What, or who, am I being tempted to worship at the moment instead of remembering the presence of God? Should I perhaps think very seriously, relationally, carefully, about what I am doing when I become erotically involved with anyone – about what it might mean for them, and for all the webs of relationships we both already have? Should I perhaps think very seriously, relationally, carefully, about the ways in which my identity is woven into the webs of relationship around me? Whose welfare do I have in mind when I decide to satisfy a desire? Is there a work of understanding I need to do in order to recognize my abusive neighbour as another human being? Are there aspects of my life for which I am thankful and do I remember to honour them?

These are the issues of stability, of living well in the place you happen to be, and a church mindful of them would look harder at, and make more visible, the reconciling example of a Jesus who says 'go home' as well as 'follow me'. Very, very few are called to leave the messy needs of their lives behind.

For if lots and lots of people *were* to take worshipping God seriously, churches would have to think about, and help people to negotiate, all this complicated stuff. Because those are the kinds of lives people would bring with them. They would not be simple to reconcile, at all. All of a sudden we would need what the early modern churches called 'practical divinity' – spiritual help in discerning how to live well in a world of complex and nuanced relational and moral choices.

But there would be one huge help in all this. Christian community is not primarily a community of kin. The bonds of love, for Christians, go beyond blood-ties; the demands of recognition don't acknowledge the boundaries of class and race, identity and tribe. So if the family, or the community, you have inherited is full of people who are 'related' by ties brought about by the historical criss-cross of chaotically satisfied desires among your own generation or another's, perhaps you begin by acknowledging that the Spirit really is asking you to take some responsibility for a person you never expected to have to love. You start from where you are. And then you listen, hard, for what may be a very unexpected command.

Our own wants are treasures

'Wants', says the mystic Thomas Traherne, 'are the bands and ligatures between God and us.'[24] He is thinking about desire as the major tie between mortal longing and its ever-present divine source. In his thought he doesn't really bother with what might be seen as the obvious point of such a tie: that it could be a direct route for the soul, taking it from lack to fulfilment. In fact, he doesn't really seem to be interested in fulfilment as an idea at all. On the contrary, he says, 'Our own wants are treasures. And if want be a treasure, sure everything is so.'

Traherne is preoccupied with the ways to notice God that are available to human experience. The 'bands and ligatures' of human boundedness to him carry a particular weight of connection. He calls it being 'infinitely obliged'. What is most sublime in being human, hints Traherne, is intimately tied up in what is most mortal, most limited.

Infinite obligation sounds like the ultimate modern nightmare: servile, abject, non-egalitarian, imprisoning, weak, all the rest

---

24 Thomas Traherne, *Centuries of Meditations*, 51, in Thomas Traherne, *Centuries* (Leighton Buzzard: Clarendon Press, 1960), p. 24.

of it. But Traherne doesn't see it that way at all. He's pointing out that obligation (the word means 'to bind') is the fundamental condition of human existence. If Traherne had known the term 'the buffered self' he would have been very quick to notice that it was a convenient fiction. Only a person insulated from the ordinary conditions of human survival within human community could ever even be tempted to take it literally.

Bonds (in the sense both of limits and of connections) are real for every person ever born. It goes as far back as you can push it. From the material stuff of which we are formed and how that forming happens, through the pragmatic limits of what the earth will give in the way of food, water and shelter, through the multitude of emotional exchanges that make up the stuff of a life, to the self-understanding shaped through the social relationships that form us, we are creatures made almost entirely by obligation, by bonds. Our limits are what allow us to participate creatively in all beauty, meaning, order and safety.

Our greatest blessings come from the things we hadn't managed to see by ourselves. 'From Eternity it was requisite that we should want,' writes Traherne. 'We could never else have enjoyed anything.' So obligation is how we live, and that is why the root of all our being is our infinite obligation to the Lord of life himself.

From the God's eye view he asks nothing of us we are not willing to notice. But in recognizing the simple truth of our infinite obligation we are, if we wish it, made free.

7

Meeting

The Lord is in this place

'No one has ever seen God,' writes the author of the first
letter of John.[1] And another scriptural letter-writer associates
God's unseeability with his eternal being. 'It is he only who has
immortality and dwells in unapproachable light,' he writes,
'who no one has ever seen or can see.'[2]

But the Scriptures are soaked in meeting God. Book after
book is driven by longing and expectation, the desire to
see 'face to face'.[3] It is true that sometimes coming close to
God overwhelms the human frame: heavy with an awe that
weakens the watcher's limbs;[4] irradiated with the dazzle of the
'unapproachable light';[5] dependent on thick cloud to protect
the fragile eye from a presence too bright to gaze upon.[6]

But often, meeting God happens within the ordinary stuff of
life. Unremarkable landscapes and domestic encounters fill up
with holiness. A fugitive who has betrayed his twin brother,
a man called Jacob, sleeps in a spot like any other and finds
God standing beside him. The way to heaven is open and full
of busy angelic traffic. He is astonished at what the ordinary

---

1 1 John 4.12.
2 1 Timothy 6.16.
3 Genesis 32; 1 Corinthians 13.12.
4 Daniel 10.4–12.
5 Exodus 34.29.
6 Exodus 24.16–18.

could hide and could contain. 'Surely the Lord is in this place', he says, 'and I did not know it'.[7]

God's holiness, and God's miracles, entreat the everyday goodness in human love and show it to be holy, to be miraculous. Years after Jacob's guilty flight, on the eve of a risky encounter with the brother he betrayed, a man wrestles with Jacob in the dark. Just before sunrise, the stranger endeavours to release himself, but Jacob holds on. He asks for a blessing – the very thing he stole from his twin. What does he want this one for? He has begged God for his life. The stranger is uneasy with Jacob's tenacity; he does not want his face to be seen in the growing light of day; and when Jacob asks his name, he evades the question. (Moses will encounter a similar evasion.[8]) But, in order to gain his release before the daybreak reveals him, the stranger grants the blessing. He keeps his own name secret but renames his opponent *Israel*, which can mean 'the one who contends with God'. Jacob, triumphant, his hip dislocated with the fierceness of the encounter, exclaims, 'I have seen God face to face.' He leaves the place just as the sun rises and goes haltingly towards he knows not what. Perhaps his own death. Perhaps something much less likely.[9]

Jacob's exclamation is not quite truthful. Though he was intimate with the stranger's shape, strength and voice, he never saw his face. He was left in the dark. He received this new blessing as trustingly blind as was his father Isaac, from whom years ago he tricked his brother Esau's birthright, the father's benediction and substance intended for the firstborn son.

Jacob limps towards meeting this long-lost brother, this old, old, enemy, carrying a blessing from someone he could not see and could not name, a blessing enclosed in an identity that describes what he already is – *Israel*, full of a stubborn, even greedy longing to possess the things of God – but re-aligned now to a fierce and difficult intimacy with God's own being.

As the estranged brothers come towards each other, Esau 'ran to meet him, and embraced him, and fell on his neck and

---

7 Genesis 28.10–17.
8 Exodus 3.13–15.
9 Genesis 32.22–32.

kissed him, and they wept'. And Jacob notices something he
has never understood before. He suddenly gets the holiness of
enduring love. Astonished, he says to his brother, 'To see your
face is like seeing the face of God.' The face he never saw in
the dark he sees now in the light. It is the face of the brother he
cheated, the brother who forgave him.

He 'ran to meet him, and embraced him, and fell on his neck
and kissed him'. The love that forgets all debts and all betrayal
echoes down the centuries from Esau's actions and finds its
way into another, more recent story of two sons. In this version, as the betraying fugitive son comes back home penniless,
hungry and sorry, his father, 'while he was still far off . . . ran
and put his arms around him and kissed him'.[10] Did the son,
astonishingly forgiven, look upon his father's face and think,
'to see your face is like seeing the face of God'? Did Jesus rely
upon his listeners picking up the echo, noticing that the wast-
rel son in need of love could even have been called a greedy
contender for his father's wealth and substance, named by that
father with the name Israel? Did they wonder why, this time,
the virtuous elder son could not at first forgive, and whether
his father's picture of a lost child found, a dead child living,
moved him to pity? Did he manage in the end to weep for his
maddening, greedy, demanding, chaotic sibling?

'Found in human likeness'

In the Old Testament, the knowledge of God in the human face
is intermittent, a matter of momentary revelation. But within
the writings we call the New Testament, the man Jesus is God
continuously manifest in the fragile, ordinary, human form.
He is nothing if not domestic. His stories are peasant tales:
housework, village life, landlords, make-do-and-mend, families. They imagine God intensely, expectantly present in these
homely spaces, eager for a meeting which people often evade
or refuse. The woman who sweeps a house to search for her

10 Luke 15.11–32.

lost change is like God seeking out a lost beloved. The household lamp blazes with sacred light. The feast-tables, heavy
with food and wine, wait for guests discourteously absent. The
father longs for his lost son to come home.

The ways that Jesus imagines the meeting of human and divine
includes the marriage metaphor, but it's one image among many
different images of human relationship he asks his listeners to
think about: overshadowed by the parent–child relationship, seen
alongside the relationship of landowner to tenant, master to servant, host to guest, magistrate to complainant, friend to friend.
The imagined world in which God moves, the world of Jesus'
stories, is socially varied and conscious of the complex interplay
of power. The real world of Jesus' own actions of prayer and
power and teaching and meeting is as diverse and complex as his
own context will provide; his sense of where virtue and goodness
make their home is often unexpected, unrespectable. He knows
that life is messy and that the decisions of faithfulness may look
very odd, even scandalous, from the outside.

Jesus' sayings and doings – including the miraculous ones,
the 'signs' – are a kind of *synecdoche,* the rhetorical figure
where a part stands for an invisible whole. These sayings and
doings, these signs, point beyond themselves. 'Look over there,'
they say. 'Go and see.' But they also point *within* themselves,
becoming profound and sacred acts: washing, eating, touching, looking, wiping, spitting, weeping, kissing, writing in the
dirt. 'Look inside this action,' they say. 'Stay and see.'

Or both at the same time, in the words Jesus uses when he
first meets two of the apostles: 'Come and see.'[11] Human desire
is where God makes himself known. Human desire is where
he is born, looked upon, adored, fed, menaced, nurtured, relinquished, met, loved, clutched at, cheated, betrayed, reviled,
tortured, killed, mourned, wept over, recognized, embraced,
remembered. It is the place where God 'emptied himself,
taking the form of a slave, being found in human likeness',[12]
risking everything to make a temporary home bound into the

11 John 1.37–39.
12 Philippians 2.7.

temporary world, and so turning every temporary home in the temporary world into the habitation of God.

'This must be the place'

I wrote this book about the relationship between holiness and desire. I took for granted that longings are immortal – completely bound into the ways that mortal human beings look out beyond the limits of their time and space, yearning for what they do not know, wanting to be fully known. I have taken quite a bit of space to think through some of the deathly uses to which desire has been put: short-term ends, immediate gratification, fast profit; the myopic, distracted, downcast eyelines of modern pleasure. I've written about 'sex' as a dominant metaphor for desire; talked about how difficult it is to define what 'sex' even is; explored the very imperfect success of modern attempts to separate the behaviours of 'sex' from the webs of relationship that make up selfhood. So a lot of this book has been about the places where mortal desire and immortal longings haven't managed to meet after all.

But they do meet.

They meet where people commit the finite time they have to someone else, giving themselves away, knowing that they can't predict what the future will be or by what violence of parting they will eventually be overborne. The fidelities of commitment are always reckless. They involve learning the difficult disciplines of forgiving and being forgiven when, as they will, the betrayals, mistakes and cruelties pile up. They make their bid for stability in the face of inescapable change. Fidelity declares that 'love's not time's fool',[13] that the depredations of age, betrayal and death are not the last and greatest power. They choose fidelity even though the full weight of loss is the place to which the faithful must travel.

---

13 William Shakespeare, Sonnet 116, line 9, in *The Sonnets*, ed. G. Blakemore Evans (Cambridge: Cambridge University Press, 1996), p. 84.

That's just the beginning of it, the crazy decision, which has quite a lot in common with the sacrificial decisions that people make every day not just for spouses but for parents, children, friends and neighbours, even for strangers, decisions that declare that love to be a stronger principle than the conservation of energy.

There is more.

The faithful make time their friend. The mortal meets the immortal when people live as if their limits were the most precious thing they could ever have. Repeating the days, the weeks and months and years, the seasons and the stages of a life in relationship with another person creates a deep bond between memory and experience. The seeing that you do when you look upon your beloved sees more than just the now of that moment. It sits just as much as in what was once there, a younger and less formed beauty still speaking and alive in the older face. In sleep, or more often in the smoothed out moments of fulfilled desire, that young face, the face that knew less and expected more, offers its untroubled lines to your eye.

Other times, harder times, sees the shadow of a person to come in the tense line of a suddenly jutting jaw, shadowed eye sockets, high colour, a defeated sag to the mouth. 'Love me till my heart stops' is what that face is saying. 'Love me till I'm dead.'[14] It asks for the kind eye to see its mortality at the same time as seeing what else is there, the complex story of a soul labouring to make sense, bound into cognition, recognition, over and over and over before the long exhale with which everything will stop.

The passing of time, and what it does to the body and the face, makes the ferociously defended distinctions between genders less and less important and less and less visible. Within the heart, other apprehensions, steadier but just as strong, take their place alongside selfish and disruptive erotic passion: the overwhelming mixture of potent feeling sometimes dismissively named nostalgia, or the mortality-reliant faculty of wonder. It

---

14 Talking Heads, 'This Must Be the Place (Naive Melody)', on *Speaking in Tongues* (1983).

is the faithfulness that is holy in relationship, not the sex; it is the particularity of attention, teaching each partner something about the exclusive tenderness of God for each fragile soul one by one.

The mixture of memory with experience, the repeated patterns that are patterns of living and patterns of praying: they don't stop when we stop. Remembering is what it says it is: it makes again what was made, it breathes life into what has been, restoring and transforming the stuff of a life: 'God has made everything beautiful in its time.'[15] Remembering is the earnest of the promise of resurrection. 'When I awake and behold your likeness, I shall be satisfied.'[16]

When we, at last, are released from the rule of time; when the face of God looks upon what we have made of the faces we have; when we, longing to know, are at last fully known; when the laborious daily acts of recognition and remembering come into the clear completion of the whole being; when the eternity we began to glimpse by watching the workings of time upon another self will be gathered up in one steady vision; when the shadowed partial gives way to a steady and perpetual shining – it will none of it be strange. We will remember all of it; ourselves being remembered, we shall be in possession of something it will turn out we knew all the time. *Do not be afraid, I am with you.*

For then, and there, beyond what then can be and what there can mean, we shall meet and never part.

---

15 Ecclesiastes 3.11.
16 Psalm 17.15.